I0130606

Using Social Emotional Learning to Prevent School Violence

Using Social Emotional Learning to Prevent School Violence is an essential resource that seeks to close the existing gap in the literature on ways to mitigate school violence, as well as to advocate for the integration of social emotional learning in schools.

In an effort to create culturally responsive, student-centered, and secure school environments, this book outlines strategies that highlight the importance of collaboration between critical stakeholders in identifying and mitigating bullying, assisting students struggling with relationship-building skills, grief and loss, and anger; particularly those that demonstrate the need for power and control or the desire for retaliation. Mental health issues are also taken into consideration. Proactive responses and best practices are exemplified in order to equip struggling students with resources that foster their well-being and success. Dr. Paolini draws upon extensive research in her depiction of school violence in America's education system and designs lesson plans and activities that address and align with each of the social emotional learning core competencies for both elementary and secondary school counselors.

This book will be of interest to critical stakeholders in P-12 settings as well as those in higher education, particularly as a resource for graduate students training to become transformative school counselors.

Allison Paolini, Ph.D., NCC, is an Assistant Professor of Counselor Education and is the Director of the MSE School Counseling Program at Arkansas State University. She has previously worked as an elementary school counselor and her main area of research interest is social emotional learning and its instrumental role in mitigating school violence, as well as the impact of social emotional learning on fostering academic, social/emotional, career readiness, and success for all students.

Using Social Emotional Learning to Prevent School Violence

A Reference and Activity Guide

Allison Paolini

Routledge
Taylor & Francis Group

NEW YORK AND LONDON

Cover image: SiewHoong (Getty)

First published 2023
by Routledge
605 Third Avenue, New York, NY 10158

and by Routledge
4 Park Square, Milton Park, Abingdon, Oxon, OX14 4RN

Routledge is an imprint of the Taylor & Francis Group, an informa business

© 2023 Allison Paolini

The right of Allison Paolini to be identified as author of this work has been asserted in accordance with sections 77 and 78 of the Copyright, Designs and Patents Act 1988.

All rights reserved. No part of this book may be reprinted or reproduced or utilised in any form or by any electronic, mechanical, or other means, now known or hereafter invented, including photocopying and recording, or in any information storage or retrieval system, without permission in writing from the publishers.

Trademark notice: Product or corporate names may be trademarks or registered trademarks, and are used only for identification and explanation without intent to infringe.

Library of Congress Cataloguing-in-Publication Data
A catalog record for this title has been requested

ISBN: 978-1-032-20096-5 (hbk)
ISBN: 978-1-032-20095-8 (pbk)
ISBN: 978-1-003-26218-3 (ebk)

DOI: 10.4324/9781003262183

Typeset in Times New Roman
by MPS Limited, Dehradun

This book is dedicated to my parents, Maris and Steven, for their unconditional love, mentorship, adoration, support, and unwavering belief in me. You are my heroes and I am supremely fortunate to have such exceptional role models. Thank you for helping me to make my dreams come true. My gratitude and love for you is immeasurable. To my son, Jordan, you have taught me what true love is. Everything I do in this world is for you. Your laughter, brilliance, goodness, humor, compassion, humility, resilience, and innate abilities are so admirable and inspire me to be the best I can be. You are my heart and soul. Thank you for being you and for choosing me to be your mom. You are pure magic. Always believe in yourself, work hard to achieve your goals, and never allow anyone to dull your sparkle; shine like the brightest star you are. Anything and everything is possible with resilience, faith, and desire for greatness. To, Coconut and Shalom, thank you for your love, loyalty, companionship, licks, hugs, and for being the most incredible fur babies. I love you both immensely. To my brother, Damien, thank you for your protection, tenacity, and strength; I love you dearly and miss you every day. To my Aunt Loris, for your courage, for being an inspiration, and for motivating me to reach my fullest potential. To my Aunt Stacy for your intelligence, drive, and adoration; you are an incredible mom, and beautiful inside and out. To my Aunt Sandy, thank you for your wisdom, love, compassion, and encouragement; you are the greatest God Mother a girl could ask for. To my Aunt Diane and Uncle Abe thank you for watching over Jordan and me and for your friendship, radiance, love, and loyalty. I love you endlessly. To my beloved grandparents, Frank, Helen, Jack, and Renee, who have taught me to keep moving forward, that after every storm comes a rainbow, and have demonstrated the importance of hard work, sacrifice, passion, diligence, perseverance, eternal love, commitment, dedication, and family above all. Thank you for being my white light and for always being in my orbit. You are my forever angels and I love you higher than Heaven.

Contents

Preface

Safe Schools

As a school counselor and counselor educator, the importance of school safety needs to be paramount. Lack of feelings of safety can lead to disengagement, truancy, disconnectedness, fear, lack of concentration, and poorer academic performance (Yahnke, 2019). Students may experience elevated levels of depression, miss classes, and have a lower GPA when they feel their safety is in jeopardy at school. Students who feel unsafe at schools may experience a higher degree of emotional issues and may be victims of bullying or violence. According to a study done at Concordia University, the researchers found that school safety was directly related to increased academic performance. Additionally, the report stated that students who do not feel safe at school or experience violence also have reported more symptoms of depression (Yahnke, 2019). Furthermore, when students feel a lack of safety at school, they are more likely to experience absence and truancy, which leads to an increase in misbehavior, risky behaviors such as substance usage, and reduced graduation rates.

Research has substantiated that students who feel safer and more protected are more successful holistically in school (Yahnke, 2019). When students feel safe at school their mental health improves, as well as do behavioral and academic outcomes. School leaders must work collaboratively and tenaciously to create a school climate that is engaging, inclusive, cohesive, celebratory, rigorous, and culturally responsive so that all students feel accepted, experience a sense of belonging, and ease. Research has substantiated that creating a positive school climate helps to reduce bullying, burnout, disengagement, and promotes cultural awareness (Zakrzewski, 2013). Creating a positive school climate also helps to mitigate absenteeism, detentions, suspensions, substance usage, as well as increases student academic achievement, augments students' motivation and desire to learn, and enhances overall well-being. According to the National School Climate Council (2007), the group identified specific components that need to be integrated in order to develop a safe school climate are as follows:

- Schools are encouraged to set norms, values, and expectations that support social, emotional, and physical safety of all students.
- Stakeholders are engaged and respected.
- Students, families, and educators work collaboratively to develop a shared school vision.
- Educators model and nurture attitudes that emphasize the benefits gained from learning.
- Each stakeholder contributes to the operations of the school and the care of the overall environment.
- Build trust between stakeholders, as that is a fundamental element to creating a safe space.
- Schools are encouraged to assess their current climate via a needs assessment in order to get baseline feedback from stakeholders, create a shared vision, and work collaboratively to fulfill the vision.
- All stakeholders must work together to create a school that is safe, supportive, nurturing, challenging, and prepares students academically, socially, and emotionally for their post-secondary endeavors.
- Provide nonacademic support services in regard to having **more** school counselors and mental health counselors in the school setting for students dealing with challenges and crises. Giving support and letting students know that they are heard, validated, and not alone is critical for their wellness.
- Augment parental and community involvement; the more parents and the surrounding community is involved, the more supported and engaged students will feel. Parental and community involvement is critical for student success.

Creating a safe environment at school is fundamentally important for stakeholder behavioral, social emotional, and academic success, as well as mental health and well-being. At the core, all stakeholders must work together cohesively to create a school climate that is inclusive, rigorous, student-centered, data-driven, nurturing, motivating, respectful, culturally responsive, strength-based, and celebratory in order to promote holistic student triumph.

Helpful Resources for P-12 Schools

Center for Safe Schools

http://www.safeschools.info/docman/cat_view/19-safe-schools-resources

School Safety

https://www.schoolsafety.gov/

Information on Crisis Planning:

https://www2.ed.gov/admins/lead/safety/emergencyplan/crisisplanning.pdf

Anti-Bullying Resources for Schools and Families

https://teach.com/online-ed/counseling-degrees/online-masters-school-counseling/bullying-resources/

No Place For Hate Anti-Bullying Program

https://www.adl.org/who-we-are/our-organization/signature-programs/no-place-for-hate

https://www.noplaceforhate.org/join-movement

Steps to Respect Anti-Bullying Program

https://youth.gov/content/steps-respect%C2%AE

Olweus Bullying and Violence Prevention Program

https://www.violencepreventionworks.org/public/olweus_bullying_prevention_program.page

CASEL School Guide

https://schoolguide.casel.org/about-casel-school-guide/

https://schoolguide.casel.org/where-to-start/

PBIS

https://www.pbis.org/

Botvin Life Skills Training Program

https://www.lifeskillstraining.com/

1 The ASCA National Model

The ASCA National Model is a core framework for school counseling programs, as it highlights and indicates the various components of a school counseling program that are instrumental for the program's success. The ASCA National Model allows school counselors to develop programs that are data-informed, delivered to all students systemically, integrate a developmentally appropriate curriculum, and work to close the achievement gap (American School Counselor Association, 2019). The ASCA National Model addresses three major domains including academic, career, and social emotional development. Therefore, school counselors work tirelessly to ensure that students possess the skills and knowledge that are needed to fulfill these competencies in order to achieve success both in school, as well as in the workforce. The ASCA National Model is divided into four parts including Define, Manage, Deliver, and Assess.

Define: There are three sets of standards that define the school counseling profession. **Student Standards** are composed of ASCA Mindsets and Behaviors for student success: K-12 College and Career Readiness for Every Student (should be capital) (American School Counselor Association, 2019). In addition, **Professional Standards** including ASCA Ethical Standards, as well as ASCA School Counselor Professional Standards and Competencies (American School Counselor Association, 2019).

Manage: In order to effectively deliver services to all students, school counselors and counseling programs must be managed in order to promote efficiency. The ASCA National Model emphasizes program focus including beliefs, vision statement, and mission statement of the school, as this helps to drive the school counseling program forward and provide structure and organization. Program planning involves the use of school data, creating annual goals, action plans, lesson plans, advisory councils, and calendars in order to plan and document time being spent on various services (American School Counselor Association, 2019).

DOI: 10.4324/9781003262183-1

Deliver: This is the heart and soul of the school counseling program, as delivery incorporates facilitating developmentally useful activities and interventions to critical stakeholders. Activities and services offered help to augment the ASCA Mindsets & Behaviors or student success in order to improve their overall academic achievement, reduce absenteeism, and enhance prosocial behaviors. According to the ASCA National Model, **80%** of a school counselors time should be spent on direct (curriculum development, individual student planning, individual/small group/classroom/crisis counseling), as well as indirect services (collaboration and consultation referral) (American School Counselor Association, 2019).

Assess: School counseling programs are fervently passionate about training school counselors to be data-driven practitioners. Data drives practice, enhances accountability, as well as allows school counselors to substantiate and demonstrate their necessity in the school setting. One of the most profound questions school counselors reflect upon is: **In what ways are students different as a result of counseling services?** School counselors must be data-driven and work intentionally to assess their program to determine its efficacy, identify strengths of the program, and areas for growth, as well as show how students are different as a result of services received within the school counseling program (American School Counselor Association, 2019). School counselors can engage in program assessment via developing annual reports. School counselors can also complete the ASCA School Counselor Professional Standards and Competencies Assessment or the School Counselor Performance Appraisal Template in order to document the impact of their services on student outcomes (American School Counselor Association, 2019).

According to American School Counselor Association (2019), the recommended caseload and student to counselor ratio is 250:1. In reality, caseloads tend to be significantly higher. As a result, counselors may not be aware of each student who may be struggling with an underlying mental health issue, dealing with bullying, anger, grief, and loss, or may lack motivation and optimism. Consultation and collaboration with critical stakeholders are vital in order to identify students who may be struggling and provide them with services. Additionally, delivering responsive services including individual, small group, classroom, as well as school-wide counseling is imperative in order to ensure that all students are receiving the resources, support, and guidance that they need in order to survive and thrive. In regard to direct services, it is essential for counselors to develop curricula that align with the ASCA National Model (2019) and specifically addresses topics and skills related to social emotional learning, as these skills have shown to play an integral role in promoting feelings of acceptance, belonging, validation, understanding, compassion, empathy, accountability, communication, diversity, self-love, love for others, and hope. In order to create school climates that are inclusive and safe, integrating character education, social emotional learning, diversity, substance usage, as well as bullying programs is imperative for the overall wellness of students personally, as well as academically.

Reference

American School Counselor Association (2019). *The ASCA National Model: A framework for school counseling programs (4th ed.)*. Alexandria, VA: ASCA.

2 School Counselors Role

Importance of Creating a Safe School Climate and Fostering Positive Relationships with Students

One of the most imperative components of the school counselors' role is to demonstrate leadership, advocacy, and work tenaciously to promote systemic change, as well as to create school climates that are safe, inclusive, and engaging in order to foster success for all students. All stakeholders must work together in order to help students feel safe, facilitate knowledge, and formulate strong and supportive relationships with students so that they feel connected and included. School climate addresses the character of a school and is based on patterns of students', parents', and faculty experiences of school. It also is representative of goals, values, relationships, and teaching practices (National School Climate Center, 2021). A healthy school climate allows for:

- Stakeholders to feel supported and safe
- Stakeholders feel respected and validated
- All stakeholders collaborate and work intentionally toward achieving the school's vision and mission
- Educators model and encourage a growth mindset; learning is not fixed and there is always room for improvement if given opportunities and resources

A positive school climate allows for enhanced academic achievement (GPA, test scores, academic performance), greater cohesion, increased graduation rates and attendance, as well as improved student learning outcomes. Schools with negative climates may have students with lower achievement scores, reduced graduation rates, bullying, and violence, as a lack of culture, community, and togetherness is lacking. According to the Safe and Supportive Schools Model in schools that have safe climates have students who feel supported, socially capable, and students who feel motivated and are challenged (American Institutes for Research, 2021). According to Education World (2011), there are a variety of ways to create a safe school environment including

- Assess the school's current climate via a needs assessment to determine the degree to which the school climate is positive

DOI: 10.4324/9781003262183-2

- Emphasize the importance of listening and collaboration
- Take a strong stance against codes of silence and encourage stakeholders with lifesaving information to come forward
- Implement antibullying programs
- Teach empathy, compassion, and resilience; we all face adversity and need to find ways to keep moving forward
- Motivate and empower students to play an instrumental role in creating a safe school climate by being respectful, treating others with dignity and compassion, encouraging leadership, involvement, connectivity, identifying similarities and celebrating differences, as well as focusing on continual growth
- Ensure that all students have a trusting relationship with at least one adult

Further, working to ensure that all students have a trusting relationship with another stakeholder is critical. Positive relationships act as positive reinforcements. When stakeholders believe in their students; they are more likely to believe in themselves. It is vital for students to have another stakeholder to talk, open up, and communicate with especially if they are going through a difficult time in order to express their feelings, as well as experience support, mentorship, and validation. Positive peer relationships, as well as positive relationships with stakeholders, are an instrumental component for reducing school violence, so that each stakeholder experiences support, recognition, inclusion, and a sense of belonging. Building positive relationships with students has also been shown to amplify student achievement, learning, and motivation, as well as shown to decrease bullying, disconnection, and violence. There are several steps that stakeholders can take to foster positive relationships with students including

- Demonstrating kindness
- Providing praise
- Building on previous successes
- Being trustworthy, accepting, and non-judgmental
- Provide structure and organization; students thrive when expectations are clear
- Incorporate humor and passion into instruction
- Display an interest in students' lives outside of school
- Share achievements with their family

Ultimately, one of the most essential responsibilities of school counselors is to work collaboratively with all stakeholders to create a school climate that promotes cohesion, togetherness, acceptance, belonging, and connectivity, as this plays a significant role in the academic, personal/social, and vocational success of all students. It truly does take a village. Additionally, formulating positive and supportive relationships with students that promote feelings of understanding, encouragement, motivation, resilience, and empowerment is critical for their well-being. According to Maslow's basic needs, on the most fundamental level, we need to experience control to feel grounded, inclusion to feel a sense of belonging, and love; to love and to be loved and experience a powerful connection with others. We have to remember that not all students with who we interact come from homes that are full of unconditional adoration and acceptance. Thus, in addition to being school counselors, we also are advocates, leaders, change agents, observers, collaborators, facilitators, champions, cheerleaders, mentors, supporters, guides, lifesavers, and those really special humans who every day make a notable difference in the lives of others.

References

American Institutes for Research (2021). *School climate*. Retrieved from https://www.air.org/our-work/education/school-climate

Education World (2011). *Creating a safe school climate*. Retrieved from https://www.educationworld.com/a_admin/safe-school-climate-bullying-prevention.shtml

National School Climate Center (2021). *What is school climate and why is it important?* Retrieved from https://schoolclimate.org/school-climate/sustainable%2C%20positive%20school%20climate,socially%2C%20emotionally%20and%20physically%20safe

3 Overview of Bullying

Bullying has a monumentally negative impact on students' academic, social emotional, and psychological well-being. Students who are both perpetrators and victims of bullying struggle both externally and internally for different reasons. Bullying is defined as unwanted, and aggressive behavior amongst children, adolescents, or adults in which there is an imbalance of power. Bullying is repeated and involves bothering and intimidating a person leaving long-lasting physical, emotional, and psychological damage (United States Department of Health and Human Services, 2015). There are predominantly three types of bullying including **verbal bullying** (name-calling, teasing threatening), **social bullying** (intentionally leaving someone out, telling others not to befriend someone, spreading rumors, or humiliating someone), or **physical bullying** (hitting, kicking, or physically assaulting someone) (United States Department of Health and Human Services, 2015). Unfortunately, bullying is one of the leading causes of gun violence in schools. Therefore, addressing bullying and implementing antibullying programs is vital for school safety. Promoting family involvement, providing education, strengthening students' social emotional skills, fostering connectivity, and intervening early on is critical.

Bullying Statistics

Bullying is a serious problem in schools throughout the country. Bullying leads to an increase in dropout rates, anger, resentment, impaired self-worth, sadness, and retaliation. Bullying affects everyone including those who are bullied, those who bully, and those who see bullying occur. Bullying is associated with a myriad of negative outcomes in regard to mental health, substance usage, and suicide (U.S. Department of Health and Human Services, 2020). One in five high school students reported being bullied on school property in the last year. Bullying is one of the most pervasive and commonly reported issues in schools. Almost 14% of

DOI: 10.4324/9781003262183-3

public schools report having a bullying incident once a week and reports of bullying are highest for middle schools (28%) followed by high schools (16%) and primary schools (9%) (Center for Disease Control, 2019).

According to the National Center for Educational Statistics (2017):

* Approximately 20% of students nationwide aged 12–18 experience bullying (U.S. Department of Health and Human Services, 2020)
* A higher percentage of male than female students report physical bullying, whereas a higher percentage of females reported being subjects of rumors or excluded from activities
* 41% of students who reported being bullied said that they thought it would reoccur
* Of those students being bullied, 13% were made fun of or insulted, 13% experienced rumors, 5% were physically assaulted, and 5% were excluded from activities on purpose
* The majority of bullying 43% has taken place in the hallway or stairwell at school, 42% in the classroom, 27% in the cafeteria, 22% outside of school, 15% online or via texting 12% in the bathroom or locker room, and 8% on the bus
* 46% of bullied students indicated that they reported the incident to an adult
* School-based prevention programs decreased bullying up to 25%; this is noteworthy, as antibullying programs are paramount in raising awareness about bullying, its effects, consequences, and have shown to assist in creating more compassionate school climates

Effects of Bullying

Students who are bullied may experience depression, anxiety, changes in sleeping or eating patterns, and a loss of interest in things they once enjoyed. Additionally, victims of bullying experience health issues, as well as decreased academic performance in regard to GPA and test scores. Additionally, students who are both targets of bullying or engage in bullying are more likely to struggle with mental health and behavioral issues in comparison to students who are only bullies or only bullied (Centers for Disease Control, 2019). Bullying can lead to injury, distress, self-harm, dropping out of school, suicide, and violence. Perpetrators are also at risk for substance usage, academic issues, and experiencing violence as they get older. Many times, youth who bully are bullied themselves (Center for Disease Control, 2019). Perpetrators of bullying may engage in bullying to exude power and control over others, as they feel a loss of control over their own lives.

References

Center for Disease Control (2019). *Preventing bullying.* Retrieved from https://www.cdc.gov/violenceprevention/pdf/yv/bullying-factsheet508.pdf

National Center for Educational Statistics (2017). *Indicators of school crime and safety: 2017.* Retrieved from https://nces.ed.gov/pubs2018/2018036.pdf

United States Department of Health and Human Services (2015). *Effects of bullying.* Retrieved from http://www.stopbullying.gov/at-risk/effects/#bully

United States Department of Health and Human Services (2020). *Effects of bullying.* Retrieved from https://www.stopbullying.gov/bullying/effects

4   Overview of Cyberbullying

Cyberbullying is a form of bullying that takes place through virtual means such as computers, cell phones, texting, and social media in which people can post, view, comment, and share hurtful information instantaneously. Cyberbullying happens when malicious, cruel, or negative information is shared about someone in regard to their appearance, behaviors, and choices and is meant to cause humiliation and harm (U.S. Department of Health and Human Services, 2017). Cyberbullying can happen through text messaging, email, direct messaging, spreading rumors online, posting unkind messages on one's own or another's social media account, breaking into one's account and saying hurtful things, pretending to be someone else, and hacking into their information with the intent of causing harm, as well as sexting or sending inappropriate pictures of a person and sharing it on social media or through an electronic medium (Cyberbullying Research Center, 2016). A very challenging aspect of cyberbullying is that it can be viewed by anyone who has electronic access. As noted by Hinduja & Patchin (2010), in recent years peer aggression has increased due to the amount of information available via technology. Over half of teens felt angry, hurt, and scared about being a victim of cyberbullying, two-thirds of tween victims of cyberbullying said it negatively impacted their self-esteem, one-third of tween cyberbullying victims said it negatively impacted friendships, and 13% of tweens who were cyberbullied said it negatively impacted their physical health (Security.org, 2020).

Cyberbullying Statistics

Cyberbullying is a major issue, as it is pervasive and can occur anywhere and anytime due to the Internet and electronic devices making it even more invasive than traditional bullying. According to statistics,

- One in five (20.9%) of tweens aged 9–12 have been cyberbullied, have cyberbullied others, or have witnessed cyberbullying (Patchin & Hinduja, 2020).

DOI: 10.4324/9781003262183-4

- Additionally, 14.5% of tweens shared they experienced bullying online (Patchin & Hinduja, 2020).
- Furthermore, according to the U.S. Department of Health and Human Services (2020), among students aged 12–18 who reported being bullied at school, 15% were also bullied online or via text.
- Due to COVID-19, people around the world including children and teenagers are spending about 20% more time on social media and 70% of parents have approximated that their kids spend at least four hours a day on social media in comparison to prior the pandemic.
- Moreover, 21% of children aged 10–18 have been victims of cyberbullying and as of January 2020, 44% of all Internet users in the United States said that they have experienced some form of online harassment (Security.org, 2020).
- In regard to the prevalence of cyberbullying on social media, researchers have reported that 31% of cyberbullying takes place on Snapchat, 37% of cyberbullying takes place on Facebook, and 42% of cyberbullying takes place on Instagram (Broadband Search, 2021).
- The main reason as to which people are cyberbullied is due to appearance (61%), intelligence (25%), race (17%), sexuality (15%), financial status (15%), and religion (11%) (Broadband Search, 2021).
- The researchers note that as children get older, the likelihood of cyberbullying also increases (Broadband Search, 2021).
- Further, 60% of teenagers have experienced cyberbullying (Broadband Research, 2021).
- 70% of teenagers have reported someone spreading rumors about them online (Broadband Search, 2021).
- 87% of young people have witnessed cyberbullying taking place (Broadband Research, 2021).
- 95% of teenagers are connected to the Internet and 5% of those teenagers are using social media (Broadband Search, 2021).

Effects of Cyberbullying

Similar to bullying, cyberbullying has detrimental effects on students' overall well-being. As a result of cyberbullying, 25% of teens said that online bullying has led to in-person confrontations. 13% of teens indicated that cyberbullying made them feel unsafe about going to school and 6% of teens indicated that their feelings had been hurt. Additionally, according to the Cyberbullying Research Center (Patchin, 2016), 64% of those who have been cyberbullied indicated that it negatively impacts their ability to learn and feel safe at school. Students who have experienced cyberbullying have more challenges adjusting to school and they are twice as likely to experience physical symptoms. Moreover, students who are cyberbullied indicated that it negatively impacted their self-worth, negatively impacted their relationships with friends and family, as well as their schoolwork (Gordon, 2021). When bullying and cyberbullying occur over and over again and people lack communication skills and coping skills, they may internalize these volatile feelings and eventually implode, potentially leading to violent outbursts.

References

Broadband Search (2021). *All the latest statistics and what they mean in 2021.* Retrieved from https://www.broadbandsearch.net/blog/cyber-bullying-statistics

Cyberbullying Research Center (2016). *New national bullying and cyberbullying data.* Retrieved from https://cyberbullying.org/new-national-bullying-cyberbullying-data

Gordon, S. (2021). Real life effects of cyberbullying on children. Retrieved from https://www.verywellfamily.com/what-are-the-effects-of-cyberbullying-460558

Hinduja, S., & Patchin, J. (2010). *Cyberbullying research summary: Cyberbullying and suicide.* Retrieved from https://cyberbullying.org/cyberbullying_and_suicide_research_fact_sheet.pdf

Patchin, J., & Hinduja, S. (2020). *Tween cyberbullying in 2020.* Retrieved from https://i.cartoonnetwork.com/stop-bullying/pdfs/CN_Stop_Bullying_Cyber_Bullying_Report_9.30.20.pdf

Patchin, W.J. (2016). New national bullying and cyberbullying data. Retrieved from https://cyberbullying.org/new-national-bullying-cyberbullying-data

Security.org (2020). *Cyberbullying: Twenty crucial statistics for 2021.* Retrieved from https://www.security.org/resources/cyberbullying-facts-statistics/

United States Department of Health and Human Services. (2017). *What is cyberbullying?* Retrieved from https://www.stopbullying.gov/cyberbullying/what-isit/index.html

5 Parental Involvement

Parent involvement is instrumental in the academic, behavioral, social emotional success, and vocational success of students. Parent and family involvement has shown to extend teaching outside of the classroom, creates a more positive experience for students, and helps to foster student success. The National Coalition for Parent Involvement in Education (2020) indicated that regardless of income or background, students with involved parents are more likely to be higher achievers, attend school more regularly, have enhanced social skills, demonstrate healthy behavior, and adapt better to school. Parents can reinforce social emotional learning skills at home including giving their children leadership roles, teaching accountability, assertiveness, communication/interpersonal skills, cultural responsiveness, conflict resolution, and emotion regulation skills so that their students demonstrate enhanced self-control and decision-making skills.

According to Chen (2020), the academic achievement of students **increases** when parents are involved and the more involvement they have, the more successful their children are in school. Further, it has been shown that parental involvement enhances teacher and school morale, as it shows that they are supportive of challenges, empathic, compassionate, and invested in their child's success. Having open communication with parents has shown to build trust and transparency, which is critical for student success, as well as building a positive and safe school climate. Schools are encouraged to work with parents collaboratively and provide resources and materials as to how they can best support their children academically, behaviorally, and emotionally. Parent involvement is especially critical in regard to mitigating school violence, as parents play a key role in monitoring their child's academic performance, emotional well-being, as well as social media accounts. If parents find alarming material or are concerned about their child's mental health, they can work with the school in order to obtain resources to best support their child.

Additionally, parents can provide insight to stakeholders about any concerns that they may have about their child, and together everyone can work together to help support and foster student growth. In order to

DOI: 10.4324/9781003262183-5

augment student success, parents are encouraged to be present when possible, demonstrate an interest in their child's work, have a positive attitude toward school, as children model their parents' behavior (Brooks, 2019).

Some Challenges that May Impede upon Parents' Involvement

According to Larsen (2019), there are certain barriers to parental involvement including

- Lack of accessibility: School communication that is only provided electronically or only in one language may prevent parent involvement
- Too many communication tools: If teachers use several different tools to communicate, this may lead to feelings of being overwhelmed or frustration
- Too much or too little communication: Clear, open, and structured communication is vital for parent engagement, therefore, limiting information from an array of sources is important so that parents know exactly where to access the information readily

Strategies that Schools Can Use to Maximize Parental Involvement

There are several strategies schools can use to increase parental involvement including the following:

Communication

- Focus on the strengths: Educators and leaders who emphasize student strengths experience greater parental involvement, as parents know that the stakeholders working with their children want them to succeed and believe in their abilities. Taking a strength-based approach is critical for student motivation and performance.
- Communicate using one tool or using a specific medium: Communication that is direct and accessible is important. Schools that use one platform to communicate with parents, will likely experience greater parental involvement. For instance, using **Google Drive** and uploading folders there that correspond to specific information can be very helpful for parents, as it is organized, structured, and in one place.

Emphasizing Accountability

- Encouraging parents to be accountable and motivating their children to complete their assignments is critical. All stakeholders need to work together in order to foster student success.

Conduct Workshops for Parents

- Facilitating workshops addressing a myriad of issues is paramount for enhancing parental involvement.
- During elementary school, counselors can facilitate workshops on character education, social emotional learning, enhancing social skills, tips on conflict resolution, or bullying.
- During middle school, counselors can facilitate workshops on peer pressure, making healthy choices, the importance of advanced placement/honors courses, human development, bullying, tips for boosting academic performance, and social emotional learning skills.
- During high school, counselors can facilitate workshops on college/career readiness, college admissions process, financial aid using NAVIANCE for college exploration, entering the military, career exploration, the importance of advanced placement/honors courses, extracurricular activities, and social emotional learning skills vital for post-secondary success.

Hold Schoolwide Events

- Having schoolwide events is an effective way to increase parental involvement.
- Having family literacy night, science fairs, parent–teacher conferences, homecoming events, or award ceremonies can all help to augment parental involvement.

Encouraging Parents to Monitor Social Media

- Most students today are communicating with their peers via social media or some electronic medium.
- Many students who are facing challenges psychologically or emotionally provide warning signs that they are struggling either through posts, drawings, letters, or messages on online forums.
- It is essential that parents are aware of what their children are posting online in order to best provide support.
- Parents spend a significant time with their children at home and are aware of changes that may be taking place academically, emotionally, and behaviorally.
- It is paramount that parents are cognizant if their child is struggling in order to be proactive rather than reactive. Parents can work with school stakeholders such as the school counselor who can implement interventions and provide resources that will best support the student.
- Using an app such as BARK can help parents more effectively monitor their child's social media postings so that they are aware of any alarming posts or concerns. BARK promotes a partnership between parents and schools and has helped augment the safety of

students nationwide by minimizing school shootings and challenges with self-harm https://www.bark.us/

Parent Surveys

- Stakeholders in today's society are data-driven. Everything stakeholders do in the schools is driven by data and feedback.
- Administering surveys or needs assessments to parents throughout the year (particularly at the beginning of the year) is critical.
- This helps stakeholders to obtain parent feedback about the issues that they believe are most pressing.
- It is monumentally important not only to obtain but also to implement the feedback in order to meet the parents' and students' needs and goals.
- Based on parent feedback, stakeholders, such as the school counselors, can develop interventions to address the issues that parents feel are having the most impact on their children.
- In order to make a difference, stakeholders must use and incorporate stakeholder feedback in order to be as intentional as possible and to address the issues that are having the greatest impact on the students' well-being.
- School counselors can develop surveys or needs assessments using Qualtrics or Survey Monkey.
- Surveys or needs assessments can be quantitative (numerically based) using a Likert scale in order to assess the degree to which a challenge exists.
- For example, if school counselors created a needs assessment to gauge the degree to which bullying occurred in their school, they could ask the following:
  - **On a scale from one to five (1 being low and 5 being high) rate the following**
  - Rate the degree to which you believe your child has experienced bullying or has witnessed bullying
  - Rate the degree to which you feel the bullying is negatively impacting your child's academic performance
  - Rate the degree to which you believe bullying is negatively impacting your child's social skills
  - Rate the degree to which you believe bullying is negatively impacting your child's self-esteem
  - Rate the degree to which you believe your child possesses effective coping skills to deal with bullying
  - If a classroom presentation or small group addressing bullying is offered in the future, rate the degree to which your child would be interested in attending

- Obtaining preliminary feedback from parents is vital, as this feedback will let counselors know the degree to which parents are concerned, as well as which topics need to be addressed in order to create a safer and more inclusive school climate

Creating Culturally Responsive School Climates

- Developing school climates that are culturally sensitive and responsive is critical for parental and familial involvement, as this helps to promote inclusivity, connectivity, enlightenment, fosters learning, and celebration of similarities and differences.
- Creating a culturally responsive climate helps parents to feel more comfortable, invited, included, and amplifies feelings of understanding, validation, as well as communication.
- Having information translated into languages other than English can be very beneficial especially for families whose native language is not English; this can further help to create openness, communication, and build trust.
- Recognizing diversity is incredibly important, we live in a very multi-faceted society and all cultures should be represented and celebrated.
- Having cultural awareness months in which various cultures are recognized can be very helpful.
- Inviting parents in to speak about their culture of origin can be another effective way to enhance cultural responsiveness.
- The Anti-Defamation League has a wonderful program addressing cultural diversity called the World of Difference Institute. This is a training for stakeholders that addresses topics such as race, ethnicity, values, ideologies, and bias. All stakeholders must work together in order to develop a school culture that is aware, accepting, and emphasizes equity for all https://www.adl.org/education-and-resources/resources-for-educators-parents-families/educational-programs-training

References

Brooks, A. (2019). *Experts discuss the importance of positive parental involvement in education.* Retrieved from https://www.rasmussen.edu/degrees/education/blog/parental-involvement-in-education/

Chen, G. (2020). *Parental involvement is key to student success.* Retrieved from https://www.publicschoolreview.com/blog/parental-involvement-is-key-to-student-success

Larsen, J. (2019). *Strategies for schools to improve parental engagement.* Retrieved from https://www.gettingsmart.com/2019/10/10-strategies-for-schools-to-improve-parent-engagement/

National Coalition for Parent Involvement in Education (2020). *What research says about parent involvement.* Retrieved from https://www.responsiveclassroom.org/what-research-says-about-parent-involvement/

6 Mental Health Statistics Within Schools

A significant number of students (children and adolescents) have undiagnosed mental health disorders. The majority of youth (75%) whose disorders are properly diagnosed are not receiving treatment. Mental health is a key component in students' healthy development (Stagman & Cooper, 2010). One in five children from birth to the age of 18 years, struggle with a mental health issue (Stagman & Cooper, 2010). One in ten youth has a serious mental health problem that is severe enough to impede upon his/her ability to function at home, school, and the community at large. According to the Center for Disease Control and Prevention (CDC), mental health disorders amongst children can impact their ability to handle emotions and cause distress. Attention Deficit Disorder, Anxiety, Depression, and behavioral issues are the most commonly diagnosed mental health issues diagnosed in children and teenagers. 9.4% of children and teens between 2 and 17 years old have been diagnosed with ADD or ADHD, 7.4% of children and teens between 3 and 17 years old have been diagnosed with behavioral challenges. 7.1% of children and teens between 3 to 17 years of age have been diagnosed with anxiety and 3.2% of children and teens 3–17 years old have been diagnosed with depression (CDC, 2021). Levels of depression and anxiety amongst children and teens have increased over time, largely to changes in society, social media, the Internet, and the pandemic. Research notes that 1 in 6 children aged 2–8 years old (17.4%) had a diagnosed mental, behavioral, or developmental disorder (CDC, 2021).

Furthermore, it has been found that boys were more likely than girls to have a mental, behavioral, or developmental disorder. Also known is that age- and poverty-level impact treatment and those at a higher poverty level will be less likely to seek treatment in comparison to their more affluent peers (CDC, 2021). These statistics are important for school counselors and mental health professionals in the schools and local agencies to be aware that mental health struggles are pervasive and impact all students of all backgrounds and ages. It is essential that services can be provided for students who may be struggling in order to help them emotionally, psychologically, behaviorally, and academically. School counselors are

DOI: 10.4324/9781003262183-6

encouraged to facilitate responsive services including individual, small group, and classroom counseling addressing anxiety, depression, coping skills, bullying, interpersonal skills, emotion regulation, conflict resolution, mindfulness, and accountability in order to educate, enlighten, and raise awareness of all students in order to help them evolve into healthy and well-adjusted beings.

Moreover, in regard to statistics regarding mental health, this is NOT to say that mental illness is directly correlated to violence. In fact, many struggling with mental health issues have experienced being victims of volatility. However, it is important to note that if mental health challenges are not addressed it can lead to disturbances behaviorally, psychologically, and emotionally. This can then lead to an increase in impulsivity, rage, deep sadness, and a loss of self-control, coping skills, and decision-making skills, which could potentially lead to violence.

COVID-19 and Mental Health

COVID-19 has had an immeasurably negative impact on the mental health of all people worldwide; especially children and teens. More than 1.6 billion students in over 190 countries have experienced major disruptions to their education and 24 million children and teens may dropout as a result of this pandemic (Roffey, 2021). Additionally, millions of children and teens worldwide do not have access to the Internet, further impeding upon learning and exacerbating the achievement gap. In addition to the negative repercussion that COVID-19 has had on academic achievement, it has had an even more dire impact on the mental health of children and teens. Since COVID-19, approximately 150 million children are experiencing poverty. Furthermore, a global study was conducted on the hidden impact of COVID-19 and children across 37 countries and found that more than 8 out of 10 children reported experiencing an increase in negative feelings, and one-third of households reported having increased violence in their homes (Roffey, 2021).

Witnessing and experiencing violence is directly correlated to increased feelings of sadness, anger, anxiety, depression, and trauma. Additionally, prolonged exposure to violence could cause children and teens to become desensitized in that it becomes more acceptable in regard to problem-solving without consequence. Students may also believe that violence can happen anywhere at any time, further exacerbating feelings of anxiety (Daley, 2017). In addition, students who witness or experience violence may present with higher levels of aggression themselves, as behavior is modeled and learned. Children and students can also be less likely to demonstrate compassion and empathy toward others. It has been found that brain development can be impacted in children especially in young children who are not able to fully process what they are enduring (Daley, 2017). In teens who are exposed to violence, the prefrontal cortex in their brain is impacted which is responsible for impulse control and reasoning. Therefore, if teens are subjected to violence, they may experience difficulties with regulating their emotions and problem solving effectively (Daley, 2017). Challenges with emotion regulation and problem-solving can be correlated to school violence, as perpetrators may act impulsively and use volatile measures to solve problems rather than working through them in a constructive and healthy way.

In addition to challenges with potential increased exposure to violence, children and teens are dealing with other mental health issues, as a result of schools being closed, social distancing, lack of in-person interaction, fear of getting the virus, fear for their family members getting sick, as well as fear of not returning to normalcy and what our "new normal" will look like. For students with pre-existing mental health conditions, the pandemic has intensified those conditions. According to a survey conducted by YoungMinds which included 2,111 participants up to 25 years of age, 83% of those surveyed said that the pandemic has made their conditions worse, 26% said that they have not been able to access mental health support, peer support groups have been canceled, and receiving any help at all can be challenging (YoungMinds, 2020). These findings are disconcerting, as it is critical that those struggling with mental health issues have access to getting help otherwise they are struggling in silence and their condition worsening, which can potentially lead to unhealthy choices and detrimental behaviors.

Moreover, in a poll conducted by Gallup in May 2020, 1,200 parents of school-aged children (K-12) were surveyed regarding their child's mental health (Calderon, 2020). The survey showed that 29% of parents indicated that their child is experiencing harm and consequences to their emotional and mental health due to social distancing and closure. An additional 14% indicated that prolonged social distancing will continue to deteriorate their children's mental health. In addition to children who are suffering due to COVID-19, their parent's mental health is also suffering. The survey showed that 22% of adults reported experiencing struggles with mental health due to school closures and social distancing. 45% of parents also indicated that being separated from peers and teachers is a significant challenge (Calderon, 2020). Although some restrictions have eased and schools are beginning to open, in addition to ensuring students are caught up academically after being out of school for so long, schools also must ensure that they are working with students to support their overall mental health. Therefore, collaboration with stakeholders and community leaders, especially with school counselors and licensed mental health counselors will be instrumental in order to best support students holistically.

Furthermore, in a separate study conducted by Active Minds, 3,239 students in high school and higher education were surveyed in April 2020 and 20% of those surveyed indicated that their mental health significantly worsened due to COVID-19. Approximately 38% of students surveyed indicated that they were having difficulty focusing on studies and experienced more stress, 74% of students indicated that they felt it was challenging to maintain a routine during COVID-19. Going to school every day provides structure and not having school negatively impacted consistency and students' routine. Additionally, the study showed that 8 out of 10 students are struggling with focusing on school due to distractions. Also, found is that 55% of all students surveyed indicated not knowing where to go for help with their mental health (Active Minds, 2020). Therefore, it is essential that school counselors and counselors in mental health settings communicate with, educate students and their families, as well as other critical stakeholders about their positions, training, role, and how they can best provide support and resources. It is vital that students who are struggling know that there is help available and there are people who they can talk to who can help them work through challenges they are facing. Visibility is the key.

Moreover, the pandemic has further exacerbated inequality in this country, due to school closures and the impact that has had on students, especially those who may be impacted by poverty. A study conducted to assess the impact of COVID-19 on student outcomes showed that the pandemic will damage months of academic gains and leave many students falling behind; particularly in reading and math (Terada, 2020). Almost 17% of students lack Internet and reliable access and for 25% some marginalized populations including Hispanics and Black students. In addition to recking havoc on students academically, it has been substantiated that the pandemic has caused mental health of students to further deteriorate. COVID-19 has been shown to worsen existing mental health issues and has led to more mental health struggles amongst children and adolescents due to social isolation, financial struggles, and having a public health crisis (Terada, 2020). Mental health issues if left untreated can lead to serious health and emotional problems, thus, getting support early on and being as proactive as possible is paramount for students' safety and well-being. Providing differentiated instruction in order to meet the needs of all students, as well as to provide an array of mental health services will be integral for student success.

References

Active Minds (2020). *The impact of COVID-19 on student mental health*. Retrieved from https://www.activeminds.org/studentsurvey/

Calderon, V. J. (2020). U.S. parents say COVID-19 harming child's mental health. Retrieved from https://news.gallup.com/poll/312605/parents-say-covid-harming-child-mental-health.aspx

Center for Disease Control (2021). *Data and statistics on children's mental health*. Retrieved from https://www.cdc.gov/childrensmentalhealth/data.html

Daley, B. (2017). Here is how witnessing violence harms children's mental health. Retrieved from https://theconversation.com/heres-how-witnessing-violence-harms-childrens-mental-health-53321

Roffey, H. (2021). The moment we are living and our hope for the future. Retrieved from https://globalfundforchildren.org/news/the-moment-were-living-and-our-hope-for-the-future/?gclid=Cj0KCQjwyN-DBhCDARIsAFOELTmSkAMYenADah0Yim7RkXP37i1n_T4GLRNjnMG19c9913ZqWiIFhcMaAgLhEALw_wcB

Stagman, S., & Cooper, J. L. (2010). *Children's mental health: What every policy maker should know*. Retrieved from http://www.nccp.org/publications/pub_929.html

Terada, Y. (2020). COVID-19's impact on students' academic and mental well-being. Retrieved from https://www.edutopia.org/article/covid-19s-impact-students-academic-and-mental-well-being

YoungMinds (2020). *Coronavirus having major impact on young people with mental health needs*. Retrieved from https://www.youngminds.org.uk/about-us/media-centre/press-releases/coronavirus-having-major-impact-on-young-people-with-mental-health-needs/

7 Background Information

School Violence

School violence encompasses any type of volatile behavior on school grounds, during a school event, on the way to or way home from school. School violence has a monumentally dire impact on feelings of safety and completely disrupts the growth and learning of students. Violence can occur ANYWHERE; no one is immune to this. It can occur in a public or private school, rural or urban, K-12, and in universities. School violence includes physical attacks, psychological violence (verbal abuse), bullying, and cyberbullying, which today is extraordinarily prevalent due to the Internet and anonymity, as well as the use of weapons to cause harm (Yahnke, 2019).

In a report written by the National Center for Education Statistics titled, 'Indicators of School Crime and Safety: 2017', the report indicates that there were 47 school-associated violent deaths from 2014 to 2015 and in 2016, almost 750,000 victimizations including theft at school. Additionally, during the 2015–2016 academic year, almost 10% of public school teachers reported being threatened by a student at their school. During the 2015–2016 academic year, about 76% of public schools provided training for teachers on recognizing physical, social, and verbal bullying behaviors and 48% reported providing training on recognizing early warning signs for violent student behavior (National Center for Educational Statistics, 2017). Moreover, the report indicated that during the 2015–2016 academic year, there were 1,600 reported firearm possession incidents at schools in the United States. The percentage of students aged 12–18 years who reported that they had access to a loaded gun without adult permission was 4% (National Center for Educational Statistics, 2017). These findings are significant in that it is essential that parents and caregivers continue to store firearms in places that are locked and inaccessible for students so that they cannot obtain a gun. Additionally, these findings show that educators and parents need to focus on social emotional learning topics in the school including decision making, conflict resolution, coping skills, and emotion regulation, as students must learn healthy and constructive ways to deal with anger and emotions rather than resorting to violence.

DOI: 10.4324/9781003262183-7

According to Stopbullying.gov, a report titled, "Stopbullying.gov" (2021), was published that indicated that about 20% of students aged 12–18 have reported being bullied nationwide. Additionally, those who were bullied said that their bullies had an ability to influence others' perceptions of them, had social influence, were larger, and had more money Stopbullying.gov (2021). Bullying is one of the **LEADING** causes of school shootings. Therefore, schools are strongly encouraged to incorporate anti-bullying programs into their schools, as well as develop zero-tolerance policies for bullying in order to address this issue, create a more accepting school climate, and ultimately reduce the potential of violence from occurring.

School shootings have taken place over the past 300 years in the United States. The earliest known school shooting took place in 1764 and was known as the Pontiac Rebellion School Massacre and only 3 out of 13 children survived (Dixon, 2005). During the 19th century, there were 49 K-12 school shootings. In the 20th century, including Columbine, there were 207 K-12 school shootings. Although school shootings are not a new phenomenon, there has been a dramatic increase as of late. Since 2013, in the past 5 years, there have been 294 school-related shootings (K-12 and universities) in the United States (Everytown, 2015). In essence, there have been more school shootings in the past five years than in an entire century. According to Koch (2012), a student living in the United States in comparison to a Scandinavian country is 13 times more likely to be killed in a gun homicide. Research has shown that minors who are obtaining guns from home carry out the majority of school shootings. School shootings do not discriminate and they are not limited to a specific demographic region and impact stakeholders from all backgrounds, religious affiliations, and socioeconomic statuses. Gun violence in schools (K-12 and universities) decimates the sense of safety and security that all students and faculty should be guaranteed in their learning and work environments (Everytown, 2015). There is no reason as to why students and faculty should ask themselves, "Will I make it home today?" when going to school and work.

The Final Report and Findings of the Safe School Initiative, written by the United States Department of Education and the United States Secret Service focused on identifying and determining pre-attack behaviors. They indicate that 69% of those using guns are between 10 and 19 years of age (predominantly in middle and high school). In terms of perpetrators' ethnicity, 76% are Caucasian, 12% African American, 2% Native American, and 2% Asian. Most school shootings are carried out alone and 63% of perpetrators demonstrated interest in violence prior to the attack. 78% of perpetrators have a history of suicidal attempts or ideations prior to the attack (Lee, 2013). This substantiates the fact that many school shooters are experiencing feelings of hopelessness, disengagement, and feel as though their major life goals cannot be achieved. Additionally,

98% of attackers experienced a major loss prior to an attack, 63% of assailants carry out an attack to get revenge and 81% of perpetrators hold a grievance against another at the time of the attack (Lee, 2013). These findings indicate that it is vital to identify and provide support to at-risk students and those who may be grieving or have unresolved anger toward another in order to further reduce violence from occurring. The *Final Report and Findings of the Safe School Initiative* assessed incidents of school violence between 1974 and 2000 and found the following (Vossekuil, Fein, Reddy, Borum, & Modzeleski, 2002):

- Incidents of targeted violence at school rarely were not sudden or impulsive acts of violence; they were premeditated.
- Other people knew about the attacker's idea and/or plan to attack before the attack happened.
- Most attackers did not threaten their targets directly before the attack.
- There is no accurate "profile" of students who carried out school violence.
- Most attackers engaged in some behavior prior to the incident that caused concern or indicated there was a need for help.
- Most attackers had difficulty coping with significant losses or personal failures.
- Many attackers felt bullied, harassed, or were attacked by others prior to the attack.
- Most attackers had access to and had used weapons prior to the attack.
- In many cases, other students were involved in some capacity.

These findings are relevant, as we know that violence appears to be premeditated, threats may be known, and perpetrators carry out these acts of violence seem to be struggling emotionally and psychologically. Therefore, it is vital that school counselors and other critical stakeholders work together to identify students who are struggling, create an atmosphere that enables sharing of information, as well as provide support to students in order to de-escalate violence from occurring.

In another study conducted by the National Bureau of Economic Research, the researchers addressed the impact of shootings on human capital and economic outcomes and found that shootings cause an increased absence rate and were more likely to be chronically absent and repeat a grade in two years following the event due to missing school. Also, found were adverse longer-term impacts on graduation, college enrollment, and post-secondary graduation, as well as employment and earnings at ages 24–26 (Cabral, Bokyung, Rossin-Slater, Schnell, & Schwandt, 2020). The researchers found that students exposed to gun violence have increased absenteeism, lower graduation rates, and lower employment rates after post-secondary graduation. Furthermore, by ages 24–26, those who attended a school where a shooting occurred earned 13.5% less compared to those who did not. The researchers estimated that this equates to approximately $115,550 per shooting exposed student (Cabral et al., 2020). The researchers also noted that 20 years after the Columbine tragedy, the number of school shootings in the United States has more than doubled. School shootings have been linked to lower test scores and reduced enrollment. According to one researcher, the COVID-19 pandemic may have reduced gun violence in schools due to closure, however, the mental health effects of the crisis could potentially lead to increased violence when students go back to in-person learning (Crawford, 2021).

Moreover, school violence is occurring at an alarming rate. According to a Youth Risk Behavior Survey administered in 2017 by the Center for Disease Control and Prevention (2019), 6% of students indicated being threatened or injured via a weapon at school, almost 9% had experienced a school fight or physical altercation, approximately 19% had been bullied at school, approximately 4% brought a weapon to school, almost 7% did not attend school due to safety concerns, and approximately 15% of those surveyed experienced cyberbullying. These statistics are staggering. The Youth Risk Behavior Survey assesses the health behaviors that trigger death, disability, or social challenges amongst teenagers in the United States and reflects data collected from 9th to 12th graders nationwide.

In 2021, there were at least 202 incidents of gunfire on school grounds leading to 49 deaths and 126 injuries nationwide Everytown (2021a). Since 2013, Everytown, for Gun Safety, has been monitoring and tracking gun violence at schools to obtain a better idea as to how frequently kids and teens are impacted by gun violence at both K-12 schools and universities. Data have indicated that gunfire on school grounds very much reflects gun violence across the country. In general, an estimated three million children in the United States per year are exposed to gun violence and witnessing violence. Kids who are exposed to violence are more likely to struggle with depression, anxiety, post-traumatic stress disorder, have difficulties in school, and are more likely to engage in criminal activity (Everytown, 2021). It has been shown that those discharging guns on school grounds often have a connection to the school. Overall, 58% of shooters are associated with the school being former students, staff, or faculty; 39% being former or current students (Everytown, 2021). Of the three shooters involved in mass shootings, 100% of the perpetrators were current or former students. Also, in accordance with Everytown (2021), 70% of mass school shooters and attempted mass school shooters were White males. Also, found is that guns used in mass school shootings typically have come from home, family, or friends. Evidence suggests that most of the shooters (74%) obtained guns from their home or the homes of relatives or friends. Everytown (2021) has also noted that there are often warning signs. Warning signs if identified early can be a way to intervene. A study conducted from 1974 through June 2000 showed that 93% of perpetrators displayed behavioral warning signs prior to an attack (Everytown, 2021). A separate study also found that from 2008 through 2017, 100% of the perpetrators showed concerning behaviors, and 77% of the time, at least one person knew about a violent plan.

Therefore, the implication of this is that more needs to be done in schools to foster student safety, and mitigate violence, bullying, and cyberbullying in order to protect and safeguard students, as well as to help them amplify their academic, personal-social, and vocational success so that they can graduate and productively contribute to society at large.

Leading Causes of School Shootings

There are several leading causes of school shootings:

1   **Bullying and Cyberbullying:** The majority of perpetrators are victims of relentless bullying and looking to retaliate. Nearly three-fourthsof all school shooters have been victims of bullying or harassment.
2   **Need for Control and Empowerment:** Many perpetrators feel a lack of control over their own lives and are seeking control in mass organized chaos. Many of these students are also looking for recognition and acknowledgment that they are desperately seeking.
3   **Non-Compliance with Psychotropic Medication or Side Effects of Medication:** Some students who have received a mental health evaluation and a diagnosis are prescribed medication, however, may not be taking the medication. Additionally, in regard to side effects, some medications may exacerbate existing feelings of rage, anger, and cause hallucinations.
4   **Anger and Revenge:** Many kids who are struggling alone may experience sadness and feelings of anger, especially if they have experienced loss, frustration, or embarrassment. This can lead to blame, which can then cause homicidal ideations, and may feel violence is a way to solve their problems.
5   **Access to Guns:** Easy access to guns either from home, a home of a family member or friend, or purchasing online without having a background check has made gun violence in schools more prevalent.
6   **Most Shooters Have Had Challenging Lives:** Students carrying out acts of violence may be struggling with diagnosed or undiagnosed psychological issues such as depression, anxiety, or paranoia. Mental health issues do NOT cause school shootings; however, mental health is a risk factor because this can impede one's ability to cope with stressors and make healthy choices.
7   **Many Feel Desperate:** According to the FBI and US Secret Services many shooters have been found to feel desperate prior to carrying out an act of violence.

8   **Feeling Like an Outcast:** Many students carrying out acts of violence may feel excluded, rejected, or left out, which can lead to increased levels of anxiety, depression, aggression, or antisocial behavior (Chatterjee, 2019). Many marginalized kids may not have a strong support system at school or at home and having a lack of social support is large risk factor. Perhaps, many of these students may feel alone, are struggling alone, were not able to ask for help, or did not receive help they needed.

In a study conducted by Alfred University, students were asked to rate 16 possible reasons as to why school shootings occurred. Their responses included the following as the most likely reasons for carrying out acts of violence; **revenge** being no. 1

- Perpetrators are looking to get revenge and getting back at those who have caused them pain
- Other students pock on them, make fun of, or bully them.
- Perpetrators may not value life.
- Perpetrators may have been victims of abuse at home.
- Perpetrators may struggle with mental health issues.
- Gun accessibility.
- May lack supportive relationship with parents/caregivers.
- Perpetrators may have witnessed abuse.
- Perpetrators may lack friends.

Perpetrator Characteristics

There are perpetrator characteristics that school stakeholders need to be mindful of in order to identify and support at-risk students. The majority of perpetrators:

- Possess a violent temper.
- Leakage: The majority of school shooters reveal their homicidal or suicidal ideations in the form of threats, predictions, or stories (Daskaloupoulou, Igoumenou, & Alevizopoulous, 2017).
- Come from a variety of families (intact, divorced, and foster homes).
- Victims of bullying and harassment.
- Many attackers have a history of suicidal ideation, attempts, or extreme depression.
- Many attackers were known to have difficulty coping with loss or personal failures (Vossekuil et al., 2002).
- Diagnosed with either Conduct/Oppositional Defiant Disorder (may disregard authority, demonstrate defiance, have rage issues, and lack regard for the impact of their actions on others).
- Demonstrate cruelty toward animals or people.

- Post threatening messages on social media.
- Display pictures of guns or weapons on social media.
- Possess an interest in or preoccupation with violence (59% of perpetrators demonstrate an interest of violence in videos, movies, or other media (Bonanno & Levenson, 2014).
- Make threats to hurt others or themselves.
- Have serious disciplinary issues (suspension/expulsion).
- Lack family support.

References

Bonanno, C. M., & Levenson, R. L. (2014). *School shooters: History, current, theoretical and empirical findings and strategies for prevention.* Retrieved from https://journals.sagepub.com/doi/pdf/10.1177/2158244014525425

Cabral, M., Bokyung, K., Rossin-Slater, M., Schnell, M., & Schwandt, H. (2020). *Trauma at school: The impacts of shootings on students' human capital and economic outcome.* Retrieved from https://www.nber.org/papers/w28311?utm_campaign=ntwh&utm_medium=email&utm_source=ntwg1

Center for Disease Control and Prevention (2019). *Preventing school violence.* Retrieved from https://www.cdc.gov/violenceprevention/youthviolence/schoolviolence/fastfact.html?CDC_AA_refVal=https%3A%2F%2Fwww.cdc.gov%2Fviolenceprevention%2Fyouthviolence%2Fschoolviolence%2Findex.html

Chatterjee, R. (2019). *School shooters: What is their path to violence?* Retrieved from https://www.npr.org/sections/health-shots/2019/02/10/690372199/school-shooters-whats-their-path-to-violence

Crawford, K. (2021). *New study of gun violence in schools identities long term harms.* Retrieved from https://siepr.stanford.edu/news/new-study-gun-violence-schools-identifies-long-term-harms

Daskaloupoulou, E., Igoumenou, A., & Alevizopoulous, G. (2017). School shootings: A review of the characteristics and psychopathology of the perpetrators. *Journal of Forensic Science & Criminal Investigation, 2,* 1–6. Retrieved from https://juniperpublishers.com/jfsci/pdf/JFSCI.MS.ID.555598.pdf

Dixon, D. (2005). *Never come to peace again: Pontiac's uprising and the fate of the British Empire in North America.* Norman: University of Oklahoma Press

Everytown (2015). *Analysis of school shootings.* Retrieved from https://everytownresearch.org/reports/analysis-of-school-shootings/

Everytown (2021a). *Gunfire on school grounds in the United States.* Retrieved from https://everytownresearch.org/maps/gunfire-on-school-grounds/

Everytown (2021b). *Keeping our schools safe: A plan for preventing mass shootings and ending all gun violence in American schools.* Retrieved from https://everytownresearch.org/report/preventing-gun-violence-in-american-schools/

Everytown (2021c). *The impact of gun violence on children and teens.* Retrieved from https://everytownresearch.org/report/the-impact-of-gun-violence-on-children-and-teens/

Koch, K. (2012). Gun violence in America. Retrieved from https://news.harvard.edu/gazette/story/2012/12/looking-for-lessons-in-newtown/

Lee, J. H. (2013). School shootings in the U.S. public schools: Analysis through the eyes of an educator. *Review of Higher Education and Self-Learning, 6,* 88–120.

National Center for Educational Statistics (2017). *Indicators of school crime and safety: 2017.* Retrieved from https://nces.ed.gov/pubs2018/2018036.pdf

Stopbullying.gov (2021). Facts about bullying. Retrieved from https://www.stopbullying.gov/resources/facts

United States Department of Health and Human Services (2019). *Bullying statistics.* Retrieved from https://www.stopbullying.gov/resources/facts#_Fast_Facts

Vossekuil, B., Fein, R. A., Reddy, M., Borum, R., & Modzeleski, W. (2002). *The final report and findings of the safe school initiative: Implications for the prevention of school attacks in the United States.* Washington, DC: U.S. Secret Service and U.S. Department of Education.

Yahnke, K. (2019). How school safety impacts student success. Retrieved from https://i-sight.com/resources/how-school-safety-impacts-student-success/#:~:text =Students %20who%20feel%20unsafe%20at%20school%20experience%20more% 20symptoms %20of,alcohol%20use%20and%20carrying%20weapons

8 Reasons for Increased School Violence

There are several reasons why school violence has increased recently. Many researchers and practitioners believe that school violence has risen due to access to weapons, media violence, bullying and cyberbullying, isolation, and mental health issues that are not addressed. In addition to these fundamental reasons, there are others including

- Lack of counselors and mental health practitioners in the school setting (demand outweighs supply).
- Lack of fiscal resources and budgeting issues that impede hiring necessary mental health professionals.
- Access to firearms without conducting extensive background checks (previous history of violence, motivation for purchasing a gun, rap sheet).
- Struggles with undiagnosed mental illness. Approximately one-half of all teenagers in the United States have some type of mental health disorder. Of those teens, about half suffer from severe mental health impairment. Although mental health disorders do not directly correlate with school violence, many perpetrators committing acts of violence are struggling with a diagnosed or undiagnosed mental health issue. Although it is important to understand that most people suffering from a mental illness are not dangerous, for those at risk for violence due to mental illness, suicidal thoughts, or feelings of desperation, mental health treatment can often help reduce gun violence (American Psychological Association, 2013).
- Lack of effective disciplinary systems.
- Lack of collaboration between critical stakeholders including counselors, parents, and faculty members.
- Lack of violence prevention programs in schools and having a disconnect between students.
- Lack of coping skills/social emotional learning skills.
- Students who may possess violent tendencies.
- Isolation, anger, or relentless bullying.
- Yearn to retaliate for their pain.

DOI: 10.4324/9781003262183-8

- Need to feel empowered, receive an acknowledgment, and experience a sense of control in organized mass chaos.
- Availability of information on the Internet.
- Violence in movies/video games; youth who are exposed to aggressive material may feel violence is normalized and become more volatile.
- Feelings of powerlessness and guns give power that perpetrators are deprived of.
- May struggle with behavioral issues that can lead to problems interacting with others and having difficulty conforming.
- Broken family relationships and children treated more harshly are more likely to become violent later on in life (Voices of Youth, 2015). Worry, disdain, inferiority complexes, and anger can all fuel volatile behavior and could develop in those who are exposed to poor parenting or chaos at home amongst family members. This can also lead perpetrators to use violence as a way to assert authority.
- Drugs and alcohol usage has led to an increase in violence due to the lack of inhibition one may experience, which can cause irrational behavior (Voices of Youth, 2015).

Furthermore, in accordance with Dr. Peter Langman, a leading expert on the psychology of school shooters, indicates that school shootings can be prevented by early identification of warning signs in terms of attack-related behavior. Perpetrators typically reveal violent intentions via talking with peers, school assignments, or online behavior (Langman, 2012).

Additionally, the U.S. Secret Service National Threat Assessment Center (2019) reviewed over 40 incidents of targeted school violence between 2008 and 2017 and shared the following revelations, which directly align with other researchers findings:

- The majority of attacks happen in middle and high school.
- 44% of attacks take place in the classroom, cafeteria, locker room, gym, hallway in 1 minute or less.
- There is no universal profile for a student attacker.
- Attackers typically have multiple motives, particularly having a grievance with another classmate.
- Most attackers use firearms most often acquired from their homes.
- Most perpetrators experience psychological, developmental, or behavioral issues.
- Many attackers had interest in violent topics.
- All attackers experienced a social stressor within their relationships.
- Nearly every attacker experienced negative home/life factors such as divorce, drug use, abuse, or criminality within the family.
- Most attackers are victims of bullying often observed by others.

- Most attackers have a history of disciplinary issues or exhibited concerning behavior prior to an attack.

https://www.secretservice.gov/sites/default/files/2020-04/Protecting_Americas_Schools.pdf

Moreover, the FBI has put together a School Shooter Threat Assessment. According to the School Shooter: A Quick Reference Guide (2018), the FBI Behavioral Analysis Unit stipulates that there is not a universal profile for school shooters. School shooters are typically methodical and structured and most attacks are planned out. The most frequent motives appear to be revenge, dominance, and control, as well as recognition (Federal Bureau Investigations Behavioral Analysis Unit, 2018). Students who suffer loss, humiliation, lack interest, possess decreased levels of resilience, struggle with depression, are isolated, experience increased recklessness, engage in substance usage, or share disconcerting messages either verbally or online appear to be most vulnerable and likely to carry out an act of violence.

In addition, according to the Federal Bureau Investigations Behavioral Analysis Unit (2018):

- 93% of attackers planned out the attack in advance.
- 93% of attackers engaged in concerning behavior prior to a violent event.
- 75% felt bullied or threatened by others.
- 68% of attackers acquired the weapon from their own homes.

In addition, examples of FBI Threat Assessment Questions that can be asked in order to determine the degree to which a student poses a risk for carrying out an act of violence include (Federal Bureau Investigations Behavioral Analysis Unit, 2018):

- What are the student's motives/goals?
- Have there been any communications suggesting ideas or intent to attack?
- Has the student shown inappropriate interest in school attacks, weapons, and or mass violence?
- Is the student experiencing hopelessness/despair?
- Does that student have a relationship with at least one responsible adult?
- Are people concerned about the student's potential for violence?

https://www.radnor.com/DocumentCenter/View/17998/The-School-Shooter---A-Quick-Reference-Guide-FBI

School Challenges

Schools face several challenges in regard to mitigating gun violence. The caseload for both school counselors and school psychologists is a concern. The American School Counseling Association (American School Counselor Association, 2019) recommends there be a 250:1 ratio of counselors to students. In reality, most school counselors have many more students in their caseload. School psychologists have 1,400:1 ratio. Due to these extremely high caseloads, at-risk students may not be receiving the support that they need in order to be healthy and successful. Additionally, there are funding and resource concerns, which impede providing the support needed to meet the demands of every struggling student. Some schools do not have the ability to integrate anti-bullying programs due to lack of funding. Additionally, policymakers in the schools may lack knowledge about creating a safety/crisis plan addressing active school shooter prevention. Further, firearms must be stored in a place that children and teens do not have access to them. In a study conducted in 2015, high school principals were asked about their perceptions about school violence and they indicated that **lack of parental monitoring, inadequate mental health services, peer harassment, and bullying, and easy access to firearms** as the main causes for gun violence in schools. Also noted that barriers to implementing firearm violence prevention practices included lack of expertise as to which practices to implement, lack of time, and lack of research as to which practices are most effective (Price, Khubchandani, Payton, & Thompson, 2015).

In addition, there may be pushback from parents. Many parents do not want their child being labeled as having a mental health issue and therefore do not provide them with the mental health assistance that they need. One in five K-12 students struggles with a mental health issue and four out of five of those students are left untreated. Therefore, it is vital for stakeholders to help **normalize** mental health so that students who are struggling with mental health issues or are bullied receive the help, resources, and support that they need to become productive citizens.

References

American Psychological Association (2013). *Gun violence: Prediction, prevention, and policy*. Retrieved from http://www.apa.org/pubs/info/reports/gun-violence-report.pdf

American School Counselor Association (2019). *The ASCA National Model: A Framework for School Counseling Programs, Fourth Edition*. Alexandria, VA: ASCA.

Federal Bureau Investigations Behavioral Analysis Unit (2018). The school shooter: A quick reference guide. Retrieved from https://www.radnor.com/DocumentCenter/View/17998/The-School-Shooter---A-Quick-Reference-Guide-FBI

Langman, P. (2012). School shooters: The warning signs. Retrieved from https://schoolshooters.info/sites/default/files/school_shooters_warning_signs_1.1.pdf

Price, J. H., Khubchandani, J., Payton, E., & Thompson, A. (2015). *Reducing the risks of firearm violence in high schools: Principals' perceptions and practices.* Retrieved from https://www.bsu.edu/-/media/www/images/news/articles/2016/01/firearmsinschools/reducingtherisksoffirearmviolenceinhighschoolsprincipal-sperceptions%20andpractices.pdf?la=en&hash=46051210E23ED3496E2E63E DD39DA0D1B362614E

Voices of Youth (2015). *Violence in schools: Causes and solutions.* Retrieved from https://www.voicesofyouth.org/blog/violence-schools-causes-and-solutions

U.S. Secret Service National Threat Assessment Center (2019). Protecting America's schools: A U.S. Secret Service analysis of targeted school violence. Retrieved from https://www.secretservice.gov/sites/default/files/2020-04/Protecting_Americas_ Schools.pdf

9   Impact of School Violence on Students and Stakeholders

Gun violence has a detrimental and an indefinite scaring impact on students and stakeholders (Beland & Kim, 2016). According to Everytown (2021), firearms are the leading cause of death amongst children and teens. In comparison to other countries, American children aged 5–14 are 21 times more likely to be killed by a gun, and adolescents to young adults aged 15–24 years old are 23 times more likely to get killed by a gun (Everytown, 2021). Everytown (2021) has indicated that gun violence manifests in different ways in American schools and shootings have created new anxieties for students. Between 2013 and 2019, there have been more than 549 school shooting incidents in the United States (Everytown, 2021). The following are short- and long-term consequences of experiencing gun violence in school:

- Sense of safety and protection is shattered.
- Experience vulnerability, rawness, trepidation, lack of invincibility, fear that is paralyzing.
- More likely to struggle with depression, anxiety, and mood disorders, and without proper treatment these issues can have a negative impact on quality of life, as well as on emotional and cognitive functioning.
- Have lower test scores; specifically in Maths and English (Beland & Kim 2016).
- Decrease in enrollment in school.
- Challenges with sleeping.
- Resistance to school.
- Inability to fully express thoughts.
- Changes in eating and sleeping habits.
- Increased anger.
- Grief and loss.
- Increase in absenteeism.
- Less likely to graduate.

DOI: 10.4324/9781003262183-9

- Struggle with PTSD (may have recurring night terrors, survivors' guilt, reliving the nightmare over and over).
- Damage to the hippocampus (memory controlling center).
- Have difficulty concentrating and paying attention.
- Increase in dropout rates or aggressive behavior.
- Struggle with peer relationships.
- Reduced ability to form and maintain secure attachments.
- Children exposed to violence are more likely to abuse substances including drugs and alcohol.
- Violence impacts physical health and can cause physical ailments.
- Long-term health impacts in regard to increases in mortality rates, suicides, and accidental deaths for those exposed to violence (Levine & McKnight, 2021).
- Increase in anti-depressant medication usage by approximately 21% (Levine & McKnight, 2021).

References

Beland, L., & Kim, D. (2016). The effect of high school shootings on schools and student performance. *Educational Evaluation and Policy Analysis, 38*, 113–126.

Everytown (2021). *The impact of gun violence on children and teens.* Retrieved from https://everytownresearch.org/report/the-impact-of-gun-violence-on-children-and-teens/

Levine, P., & McKnight, R. (2021). *Lasting effects of exposure to school shootings.* Retrieved from https://econofact.org/lasting-effects-of-exposure-to-school-shootings

10 Role of Stakeholders in Mitigating School Violence

Although this is a complex issue that requires all stakeholders to collaborate, consult, and work together cohesively to create a secure climate,
school counselors play an instrumental role in mitigating gun violence.
School counselors are leaders, advocates, change agents, and consultants
who bridge all stakeholders together to ensure the academic, personal/
social, and vocational success of all students. There are several things that
can be done to reduce gun violence in schools (Everytown, 2021):

Acknowledge Gun Violence in Schools is Problematic

- We must address that gun violence is problematic.
- Effective school safety plans MUST involve a proactive effort to
  enact meaningful gun violence prevention policies that promote
  intervention before carrying out acts of violence (Everytown, 2021).
- Schools are encouraged to create safe climates, provide counseling
  and mental health services, and intervene prior to the violence.

Enact Secure Firearm Storage Laws, Enforce, and Raise Awareness

- The most common sources of guns used in school shootings come
  from a perpetrator's home or another's home who they know.
- States can enact and enforce secure firearm storage laws. These laws
  require that people store firearms safely what they are not in their
  possession in order to prevent unauthorized access.
- If a person accesses a firearm and causes harm, the person who failed
  to secure the firearm may be liable (Everytown, 2021).

Raise the Minimum Age To Purchase Firearms to 21

- Everytown (2021) believes that if the federal government raises the
  minimum age to purchase a gun or rifle to 21, this will help to reduce
  the number of school shootings.
- Minimum age laws can work alongside Extreme Risk Laws to reduce
  access to firearms to those who pose risk and to those under 21.

DOI: 10.4324/9781003262183-10

Require Background Checks on All Gun Sales

- Everytown (2021) recommends that all states and federal government act to pass laws that require background checks on all gun sales so that shooters cannot easily purchase firearms.
- An Everytown investigation showed that as many as 1 in 9 people looking to purchase a gun on Armslist.com are people who can NOT legally have firearms.
- Background checks are vital, as they are an effective way to prevent minors and people who pose a risk from having guns.

Steps that schools can take to reduce gun violence and promote a protected school climate are as follows:

Adopting Physical Security Measures

- Implement security measures including surveillance cameras, guards, and metal detectors.
- Place cameras in hallways, classrooms, stairwells to monitor behavior.
- Having security guards at the school can help to identify, as well as respond to dangerous situations immediately.
- Have internal door locks so that students and educators do not have to leave the classroom to lock their doors.
- Have lockdown drills in order to educate students and faculty about protocol if a school shooting were to occur. Drills should not include simulations and should be announced to students and faculty prior to the start of a drill.
- Have resource officers at schools, as they are trained to diffuse potentially violent situations (Everytown, 2021).

Create a Safe Climate (Bray, 2016)

- Inclusive, motivating, rigorous, strengths based: Counselors are encouraged to identify students' strengths and integrate strengths into setting S.M.A.R.T. goals.
- Conduct a needs assessment in order to obtain baseline feedback regarding stakeholders' perceptions of the school climate. This will tell counselors the aspects they need to foster in the school setting.
- Reinforce positive constraints including academic success, positive relationships, support mentorship, parental involvement, and engagement.

Develop Bullying Prevention Programs

- Implement policies to prevent violence such as zero-tolerance policies for those who choose to act in a violent manner.

- Address reasons for bullying.

  - Long-term consequences of bullying (low self-worth, mutilation, and anxiety).
  - Support nurturing climate/hang anti-bullying posters in the school as a way to create a more inclusive climate.
  - Outline behavioral expectations and emphasize inclusion, communication, connectivity, and respect.
  - Incorporate anti-bullying programs.

    - Olweus bullying program
    - Steps to respect anti-bullying program provide lesson plans that can be implemented in conjunction with character education topics such as respect, responsibility, citizenship, kindness in order to reduce bullying.
    - Anti-Defamation League (ADL): The ADL has two programs: *No Place for Hate*, which emphasizes the importance of having a zero-tolerance policy for bullying. The ADL will send schools decorations, banners, and lessons that can be implemented school-wide in order to create a safe school climate. Additionally, the *Diversity Institute* is a two-day training for students and parents that address cultural responsiveness, tolerance, acceptance, race, ethnicity, and ideologies. Students who attend are trained to become student ambassadors and work to create a culturally responsive and inclusive school climate.

Facilitate Training Programs/Workshops for Stakeholders (Yahnke, 2019)

- Educating faculty about warning signs is critical for reducing school violence.
- Almost half of all perpetrators of violence provide warning signs BEFORE carrying out an act of violence such as a note or making a threat (Center for Disease Control, 2019).
- Homicide is the second leading cause of death amongst children 5–18 years old.
- Firearms used in school shootings are primarily from the perpetrator's home.
- Conduct workshops for stakeholders addressing social withdrawal, poor academic performance, integrating violence in writings/drawings, anger/rage, bullying behaviors, discipline issues, substance usage, or threats of violence.
- Being mindful of these early warning signs can help stakeholders be proactive rather than reactive and provide support to students who are struggling.

Remain Visible

- Counselors must be present throughout school so students feel safe disclosing to stakeholders, as visibility helps to build trust.
- Counselors are encouraged to promote relationships with all stakeholders in order to unify the school.
- Counselors are encouraged to go into the classrooms, faculty lounge, cafeteria, and community in order to forge strong relationships with all critical stakeholders.
- Visibility is key for communication; when stakeholders feel as though they can trust you, they are more likely to open up and share information about their own personal struggles or others who may be struggling.

Identifying and Reaching Out to At-Risk Students

- Identify students who have the potential to act violently.
- Check-in, eat lunch with, help them connect with peers, provide leadership roles, and connect to community volunteer projects so these students experience a sense of purpose, belonging, and connectivity.
- Provide counseling in order to offer support, guidance, and mentorship to at-risk students.

Threat Assessments

- Need to be collaborative and all stakeholders must be involved when conducting a threat assessment, as each person will have additional insight to provide regarding the degree to which a student may pose a threat to themselves or others

  - Does the student have a plan?
  - Do they have weapons to access?
  - Do they have a support system?
  - Have they had exposure to trauma?
  - Have there been major disciplinary issues?
  - Do they have any complaints/gripes with other students or faculty? Do they appear depressed?

Increase Parental Involvement

- Set high expectations to enhance intrinsic and extrinsic motivation, promote autonomy and self-sufficiency, as well as communication.
- Stakeholders and parents need to speak openly with students to determine whether they are struggling or if they know someone who is struggling.
- Creating partnerships with parents is vital for student success.
- Schools can work with parents on educating them about bullying and warning signs of school violence.

Break Down Codes of Silence

- Encourage students who have information to come forward anonymously.
- Counselors can create a Worry Box, which acts as a method for students to record their worries anonymously so that they do not experience fear of retaliation. Students can write their names down or may choose not to and let the counselor know their concerns.

Monitor Social Media Accounts

- 55% of kids aged 12–13 and 82% of kids aged 14–17 use social media.
- Many students post messages about emotions, mentality, threats, and plans rather than verbally expressing their thoughts.
- Parents/guardians and peers need to be mindful of inappropriate postings so that they can alert administrators or authorities in order to take proper precautions and help the struggling student.
- School districts can partner with monitoring companies to track students' postings and hold them accountable (Wallace, 2014).

Provide Mental Health Support

- In order to promote more positive student outcomes and experience a reduction in violence, schools must ensure that there is adequate mental health support provided to them.
- Schools are encouraged to have social workers, school counselors, school psychologists, and mental health practitioners who can provide mentorship and guidance to students who may be struggling.
- School mental health professionals are a paramount resource for students to process challenges regarding emotional, behavioral, and social development.
- School mental health professionals can serve as key points of intervention and information gathering for conducting threat assessments and can share their experience of interactions with the at-risk student.
- Currently, school counselors on average handle 442 students (Everytown, 2021). The American School Counselor Association recommends no more than 250 students. To protect schools, there needs to be more mental health professionals hired at each school in order to more effectively serve students.

Responsive Services

- School counselors are encouraged to integrate responsive services in order to meet the needs and goals of students. Conducting individual, small group, and classroom counseling addressing mental health and social emotional learning topics is INSTRUMENTAL in reducing gun violence.

- Facilitating individual, small group, or classroom counseling addressing social emotional learning topics including bullying, depression, anxiety, grief and loss, anger management, problem-solving, coping skills, conflict resolution, leadership, accountability, assertiveness, emotion regulation, and college/career readiness are critical in order to educate, raise awareness, promote inclusivity, connectivity, motivation, as well as to provide support to students.

Mental Health Screenings

- Identification, evaluation, and referral are critical.
- Allows schools and agencies to collaborate and provide students with helpful and useful resources.
- Important to recognize that the majority of people struggling with a mental illness are not dangerous.
- No direct correlation exists between mental health issues and gun violence.

  - However, the majority of perpetrators who carry out acts of violence are struggling with a mental health issue that is either diagnosed or undiagnosed prior to the attack and if not treated, this could lead to unhealthy choices and poor decision-making.

- Mental health treatment and screenings can help to prevent gun violence for many individuals who have suicidal thoughts or feelings of depression (American Psychological Association, 2013).

Collaborating: Agencies and Law Enforcement

- School counselors **cannot** diagnose students and must refer out to mental health clinicians who can then diagnose and treat collaboratively, with psychiatrists, if necessary.
- Must refer students who pose a risk to agencies and provide resources for family members in order to educate, normalize, and raise awareness.
- Collaborating with law enforcement is key so that proper protocols can be followed in regards to preventing a crisis and if there is a potential threat, officers can have an increased presence at the school.
- Law enforcement officials need to be notified if there are threats being made of any nature so that they can be visible and proactive rather than reactive.

Develop a Crisis and Emergency Plan
- Schools must have a crisis/emergency plan if one occurs.
- Plans teach personnel how to respond or mitigate dangerous situations.

- Having a step-by-step plan is necessary so that all stakeholders know what to do if and when a crisis occurs.
- Sections need to address: Preventing, Preparing, Responding, And Recovering.
- In regard to Prevention, encourage input from all faculty members, determine those responsible for overseeing violence prevention, assess school's current protocols, reach out to students who are struggling.
- In regard to Preparedness, review current crisis plan, develop procedures for communicating protocols, establish ways to account for students.
- In regard to Response, determine the type of crisis that is occurring, determine whether evacuation is needed, decide if supplies are needed to assist.
- In regard to Recovery, providing consistency and structure is imperative. Monitor students to assess the emotional impact of the situation, identify follow-up interventions, provide time for healing.
- https://www2.ed.gov/admins/lead/safety/crisisplanning.html

References

American Psychological Association (2013). *Gun violence: Prediction, prevention, and policy*. Retrieved from http://www.apa.org/pubs/info/reports/gun-violence-report.pdf

Bray, C. (2016). *The counselor's role in ensuring school safety*. Retrieved from http://ct.counseling.org/2016/08/counselors-role-ensuring-school-safety/

Center for Disease Control (2019). *School-associated violent death study*. Retrieved from https://www.cdc.gov/violenceprevention/youthviolence/schoolviolence/SAVD.html

Everytown (2021). *Keeping our schools safe: A plan for preventing mass shootings and ending all gun violence in American schools*. Retrieved from https://everytownresearch.org/report/preventing-gun-violence-in-american-schools/

Wallace, K. (2014). *At some schools, 'Big Brother' is watching*. Retrieved from https://www.cnn.com/2013/11/08/living/schools-of-thought-social-media-monitoring-students/

Yahnke, K. (2019). How school safety impacts student success. Retrieved from https://i-sight.com/resources/how-school-safety-impacts-student-success/#:~:text=Students%20who%20feel%20unsafe%20at%20school%20experience%20more%20symptoms%20of,alcohol%20use%20and%20carrying%20weapons

11 Social Emotional Learning Overview

Social emotional learning (SEL) is the process by which children and adults obtain, apply, and execute the knowledge, attitudes, and skills necessary to understand, regulate, be in control of emotions, to set and achieve positive and strength-based goals, to demonstrate empathy for others, develop positive relationships, and make healthy choices (CASEL, 2021). SEL helps to foster equality through family and school partnerships that emphasize the importance of building trusting relationships, challenging and meaningful curriculum, and ongoing evaluation in order to ensure that students' goals and needs are being met. SEL works to empower students and faculty to create healthy, inclusive, and safe schools. School-wide SEL includes the entire school community in developing caring, motivating, and equitable climates that work to foster social, emotional, behavioral, and academic growth.

Some of the overarching goals of SEL are to enhance student self-awareness, self-management, and emotion regulation, as well as decision-making skills. Additionally, augmenting students' attitudes and beliefs about self, others, and school is integral. By doing so, this provides a strong foundation and allows for better adjustment, enhanced academic performance, improved social behaviors and peer relationships, fewer disciplinary issues, less stress, increased attendance, better graduation rates, as well as higher grades and test scores (CASEL, 2021). When students are engaged, connected, experience healthy relationships with peers and staff, enjoy coming to school, experience a sense of belonging and acceptance, are performing better in school, have a strong support system, are more in control of their behaviors, and make healthier choices, they are less likely to struggle with mental health issues, more likely to experience enhanced performance, and less likely to engage in volatile or destructive behaviors.

Furthermore, SEL skills can be taught. SEL reiterates the importance of having a growth mindset in that skills and knowledge are not fixed but can be amplified if given resources and opportunities. Research has shown that SEL programs and skills can foster and improve students'

DOI: 10.4324/9781003262183-11

connection to their school, improve behavior, as well as academic achievement (Durlak, Weissberg, Dymnicki, Taylor, & Schellinger, 2011). In a study conducted to assess the efficacy of SEL, 213 school-based SEL programs that involved 270,034 K-12 students were analyzed. The findings showed that the students who learned SEL skills demonstrated improved SEL skills, behaviors, attitudes, and academic performance. In fact, participants' academic achievement was increased by 11 percentile points. The findings further demonstrate the positive impact that SEL programs have on student achievement and wellness. Critical school stakeholders can integrate SEL competencies into their curricula in order to help students enhance their SEL skills. The researchers indicated that students who possess a higher degree of self-awareness (SEL competency), these students demonstrated increased confidence, were more motivated, and displayed resilience when faced with difficulties. Also found is that students who set high goals and are more in control are better able to manage stress, be more efficient, and obtain better grades. Further, the researchers found that interpersonal, instructional, and environmental supports lead to better school performance via having higher expectations for success, caring teacher and student relationships, experiential and engaging teaching approaches, and safe school climates (Durlak et al. 2011). Thus, through creating trusting relationships with students, by demonstrating belief in them, by developing rigorous material that is practical and application based, and by believing in students' and their abilities, this directly has helped to enhance student outcomes, as well as helped to create more peaceful and safer school climates.

According to CASEL (2021), some SEL programs addressing substance usage, violence prevention, and character education that help to develop safe, compassionate, and engaging school climates that have shown to enhance student attendance, attachment to school, motivation for learning, as well as augment academic achievement. Research has indicated that the quality of teacher and student interactions, as well as instructional practices, are vital predictors for student performance and social adjustment (Hamre & Pianta, 2007). Therefore, in order to build safe schools, to reduce school violence, and to amplify student performance, it is paramount that stakeholders work diligently to build healthy relationships with students, as well as integrate relevant teaching practices into pedagogy, as this has shown to reduce school violence, enhance student achievement, and improve the overall school climate.

SEL Principles

Teaching SEL is vital, as researchers and educators are aware of the connection between academic performance and SEL and how attending to multiple facets of student learning helps to develop and educate the whole child. In order to foster a positive school climate and help students maximize their growth, SEL guiding principles must be integrated into the curricula in order to foster student success. The first principle focuses on creating. In regard to integrating SEL into curricula, educators must **create** nurturing, caring, and safe climates for students (McGraw Hill, 2017). Stakeholders are encouraged to develop inclusive, challenging, and safe climates for students to share, problem-solve, learn, and grow. The second principle emphasizes integrating. Educators are encouraged to **integrate** SEL competencies and skills into their curricula in order to give students time and the ability to practice skills learned. Giving students opportunities to collaborate, work in small groups, communicate, manage stress, regulate emotions, resolve conflict, display optimism, and engage in perspective sharing is key for their success. The third guiding principle is communicating. Students must learn how to actively listen, respond, validate, show understanding, and express themselves in a healthy manner. This is exorbitantly important today, as most students are communicating via social media or electronically rather than having face-to-face interaction. We must teach students how to talk to one another so that they feel heard. Additionally, educators are encouraged to **communicate** with stakeholders, students, and parents, and the importance of SEL and its impact on student success. The fourth principle addresses instruction, in order for students to learn the concepts they must be taught how to apply them. Stakeholders are encouraged to set expectations, model behavior, and give students an opportunity to practice skills learned. Educators are encouraged to **instruct** on SEL and provide clear guidance to ensure that students understand SEL concepts and content via role plays, dyad work, small group experience, as well as to engage in reflective practice so that students can assess for areas of growth, as well as areas that necessitate improvement. The fifth principle addresses empowerment. Educators are also encouraged to **empower** students to learn and improve their SEL skills in order to feel a sense of pride, confidence, competence, and pride (McGraw Hill, 2017). It is important for students to feel in control, empowered, and motivated to work toward self-actualization in reaching their fullest potential, to build upon their skills, and to continue to make improvements in order to further augment feelings of competence and self-efficacy.

Moreover, students who possess SEL skills experience a decrease in dropout rates, reduced behavioral issues, fewer mental health struggles, are more resilient and better able to overcome challenges (CASEL, 2021). School counselors are encouraged to integrate SEL into their comprehensive counseling programs to make sure that students possess strong leadership skills, collaboration, problem-solving, communication, and interpersonal skills essential for their post-secondary success (American School Counselor Association, 2012). It is vital that school counselors work to create a school atmosphere that is challenging, inclusive, engaging, and promotes success for all. Research has shown that support school climates help students to feel more connected, supported, engaged, and safer (Berg, Osher, Moroney, & Yoder, 2017).

The National School Climate Center (NSCC) indicates a school climate is a "pattern of school life experiences that highlights norms, values, goals, interpersonal relationships, learning, teaching, leadership practices, and organizational structures" (National School Climate Center, 2012). Thus, in order to create safe climates counselors can integrate SEL in order to foster the overall health, development, feelings of safety and belonging, connectedness, support, and engagement amongst stakeholders (Osher, Cantor, Berg, Rose, & Steyer, 2017). In order to foster learning and social development, it is integral to create school climates that are engaging, collaborative, culturally responsive, collaborative, and focus on communication and inclusion (Osher et al., 2017).

SEL Competencies

The ASCA School Counselor Professional Standards and Competencies identify the mindsets and behaviors school counselors need to meet the demands of the school counseling profession and K-12 students (American School Counselor Association, 2019). These standards help to make sure that school counselors develop comprehensive counseling programs that address the academic achievement, career planning, and social emotional development of all students. Mindsets standards include beliefs school counselors have regarding student success and achievement. The Behavior standards address essential behaviors school counselors display via implementing the school counseling program including direct and indirect services, as well as assessment and planning (American School Counselor Association, 2019). The ASCA Mindsets and Beliefs are reflective of SEL in that there is an emphasis on growth mindset; that all students can learn and succeed, every student should be prepared for post-secondary endeavors, school counseling programs amplify student academic, career, and SEL outcomes. In direct alignment with the ASCA National Model (2019), each of the SEL competencies helps to augment students' academic, career, and social emotional skills.

SEL is composed of five competencies including self-awareness, self-management, social awareness, relationship skills, and responsible decision-making.

Self-awareness addresses one's awareness on how one's behavior impacts others. It also provides people with an understanding of one's own emotions, thoughts, ideologies, beliefs, values, and how they directly impact one's behavior. Self-awareness also includes one's ability to recognize strengths, areas for growth, as well as provide a sense of direction and purpose (CASEL, 2021). Self-awareness includes integrating personal and social identities, one's cultural background, emotions, honesty and integrity, values and ideologies, examining biases and how those impact our thoughts and relationships, one's self-efficacy and belief in themselves to reach their fullest potential, having a growth mindset and recognizing that knowledge can be expanded through opportunities and practice, as well as developing interests and having a purpose (CASEL, 2021). Self-awareness skills are important for students to possess in order to reduce violence in schools so that students are aware of their thoughts, how they are feeling, are better able to communicate their emotions, feel a sense of accomplishment, are goal-oriented, are more focused, proud of their accomplishments and attributes, and are driven toward excellence.

Self-management entails one's ability to manage and regulate behaviors, emotions, and thoughts in various situations to achieve goals (CASEL, 2021). Self-management skills are vital, as they enable students to be more in control, to think before acting, and to be proactive rather than reactive. Self-management skills allow people to delay gratification, better manage stress so they feel less overwhelmed and accomplish goals. Self-management involves managing one's emotions, using stress management, techniques, displaying discipline and motivation, demonstrating organization and structure, and bravery to make changes. Self-management skills are vital to teach students in order to reduce violence in schools so that students are more in control of their behaviors, are better able to cope, are less impulsive, demonstrate more proactive behaviors, and are able to regulate and process their feelings verbally rather than in a volatile way.

Social awareness involves the ability to understand others' perspectives and to empathize with others including those from different backgrounds and cultures. This involves the ability to feel compassion, empathy, and to recognize family, school, and community resources/supports (CASEL, 2021). Social awareness emphasizes seeing things from a myriad of perspectives, recognizing strengths and motivating others, showing concern for others, expressing gratitude, celebrating diversity, and demonstrating cultural responsiveness. Social awareness is critical for reducing violence in schools, as this helps to enhance perspective-taking, inclusivity, connectivity, and engagement for all. This helps to minimize isolation and withdrawal and works to ensure that all students feel supported, have a sense of cohesion, are understood, heard, and are important. Social awareness allows for connections to be built and helps students to feel safe, accepted, and have a sense of belonging. Social awareness helps to reduce bullying and augment empathy, compassion, and caring; all vital components for safe school climates.

Relationship skills give people the ability to establish and maintain healthy and supportive relationships and to navigate settings with diverse individuals and groups (CASEL, 2021). This involves the ability to communicate clearly and effectively, to listen actively, to work collaboratively to problem-solve conflict, to provide leadership, and perhaps most importantly; to offer help when needed. Relationship skills involve communicating effectively, developing healthy relationships, demonstrating cultural responsiveness, working collaboratively, resolving problems in a healthy way, displaying leadership, seeking and offering support, and standing up for others. Having strong relationship skills is essential for reducing violence in schools in that this allows students to communicate more effectively and talk about their feelings rather than internalize them, as well as allows students to determine ways to peacefully problem-solve in order to get to a win–win outcome. Rather than using violence, students are encouraged to talk about ways to resolve a conflict collaboratively by listening to one another's perspectives and finding a resolution. Relationship skills are also critical to possess, as these skills allow students to be more culturally aware, act as leaders in the school setting, be more understanding of one another, and be more supportive. This is very important when reducing violence in schools, as relationship skills allow students to be there for one another if someone is struggling. Thus, if a student is facing emotional challenges, that student feels as though others understand them and are there to help them as a team rather than feel alone, isolated, and misunderstood. It has been substantiated that **revenge and retaliation** are the leading causes of school shootings. Therefore, if students enhance their relationship skills, this will help them to problem-solve and have both people involved be a part of the problem-solving process, are accountable, and figure out collaboratively how to move forward in a more positive direction so that the desired outcome is reached hopefully eliminating desire of revenge or retaliation.

Responsible decision-making involves the ability to make healthy choices about personal behaviors and social interactions in diverse settings. This involves the ability to consider ethical standards and safety concerns and to assess the benefits and consequences of various actions for personal and social well-being (CASEL, 2021). This involves demonstrating open-mindedness and seeing things from various perspectives, identifying solutions for problems, assessing the consequences of one's actions, recognizing how critical thinking is useful, and reflecting on one's own role to promote personal and community well-being (CASEL, 2021). Responsible decision-making skills are monumentally important in regard to reducing school violence, as these skills allow for people to think about their choices, their actions, and the short- and long-term consequences of their actions before carrying out a decision. Responsible decision-making skills foster open-mindedness, which is essential, as this skill will enable students to see things from others' perspectives. Thus, if a student is struggling then other students will be able to help that student feel validated, as well as help that student to problem-solve collaboratively rather than in isolation. Additionally, responsible decision-making skills allow for students to be able to weigh the pros and cons of choices and to be proactive rather than reactive, and think about the potential consequences of their choices before acting out. This is vital for reducing school violence, as students who may be struggling will have the ability and opportunity to think about healthy ways to deal with their thoughts and emotions rather than making an impulsive or destructive choice and keep their welfare, as well as the welfare of others protected.

Furthermore, there is a direct correlation between SEL, school-wide practices, and parent/community partnerships. The more that schools and stakeholders integrate SEL into their instruction and the more collaboration between schools, the community, and parents, the more students will excel and master SEL skills, as they will have the opportunity to learn and execute knowledge learned both at school and at home. There needs to be consistency. The more parents and caregivers are involved, the more that they can learn ways to provide their children with opportunities to demonstrate SEL skills at home including assertiveness, communication, leadership, decision-making, and emotion regulation.

SEL Intrapersonal and Interpersonal Skills

There are key interpersonal and intrapersonal skills that SEL is comprised of. These skills enable perspective sharing, communication, validation, as well as enable people to have a better understanding of themselves and others. Intrapersonal and interpersonal skills are vital for collaboration, communication, understanding, inclusivity, connectivity, accountability, self-worth, hope and optimism, problem-solving, and efficiency. Prosocial skills are significant to possess, as they allow people to problem-solve in a collective manner, as well as promote healthy interaction with others in a way that is respectful and flexible so that each person feels understood (Jones et al., 2017).

Intrapersonal skills are skills that a person possesses that enable them to identify and build upon strengths and areas for growth, as well as to promote evolvement and self-awareness. Intrapersonal (within one self) are the intrinsic abilities one has to deal with emotions, cope with challenges, and learn information. These skills related to emotional intelligence, one's intuition and perception (Healthline, 2021). People who possess strong intrapersonal skills usually are more effective at managing behaviors and emotions, can overcome challenges, and continue to work to achieve goals regardless of distractions. Intrapersonal skills include the following:

Adaptability: Being flexible in a situation and being able to change at a moment's notice while remaining centered and in control (CASEL, 2021). Adaptability is important, as plans can change and students need to be able to adjust accordingly and demonstrate flexibility and openness to do so.

Self-confidence: Belief in oneself and in one's abilities. Self-confidence is critical for students to possess, as self-efficacy and self-confidence provide students with the ability to believe in themselves and their innate abilities. Students who feel good about themselves are more likely to perform well in school, demonstrate kindness and compassion, include their peers, and motivate others to achieve greatness. Educators can help students to enhance their self-worth by

- Focusing on their strengths.
- Providing constructive feedback, as there is always room for growth.
- Encourage students to identify strengths and what they love about themselves.
- Set realistic expectations that are congruent with strengths.
- Encourage teachable moments. Even if students do not experience the outcome they are hoping for, they can still learn, grow, and become stronger and wiser as a result of the experience.

Self-confidence is critical for reducing bullying and school violence because students who are confident are not as susceptible to allow others' comments to impact them, as they have unconditional love for themselves. Additionally, when students are confident they do not have a need to hurt others because they feel good about themselves and want others to thrive, as well. Therefore, it is vital for educators to work to boost the confidence level of all students so that everyone feels encouraged, recognized, and proud.

Emotion regulation: Being able to manage emotions and remain in control. Emotion regulation allows students to have control over their behavior and to remain actively engaged. Emotion regulation also allows students to avoid negative emotions and to foster positive ones (Fried, 2011). According to We Are Teachers (2018), Educators can help students to enhance their emotion regulation by

- Showing students that emotions drive behaviors. Talking about emotions is helpful in order to identify how one is feeling and then to process healthy ways to deal with that emotion.
- Being patient. Many times kids who struggle to manage their emotions are falling behind academically. Therefore, educators can work with students to identify the root cause of issues by teaching emotions and being patient, as this takes time.
- Helping students to understand emotions in real-time so that they are able to recognize emotions, as they are experiencing them.
- Having a calm down corner in the room with play-doh, soft music, tangible objects that students can use, do deep breathing, and learn to de-escalate emotions by themselves.
- Using the emotion freedom technique to tap on the acupressure point in order to alleviate tension/stress and display greater self-control.

Emotion regulation is vital for reducing bullying and violence, as students have greater self-control, are able to think before they act, are able to think about the consequences of their behavior, and are able to demonstrate restraint and make sound choices.

Openness to new ideas: To be open to learning, growing, evolving, and seeing things from various perspectives. Openness to new ideas is an important intrapersonal skill for students to possess, as this is what fosters learning and growth. It is vital for students to be able to see things from different vantage points and a myriad of perspectives, as this helps to augment awareness of self and others. Openness to new ideas also helps to improve performance, motivate students, promote empathy, and enable students to see things from others' points of view, which is pivotal for learning, acceptance, growth, and understanding.

Time and stress management: Time and stress management involve managing time effectively in order to avoid experiencing procrastination and stress. Time and stress management are integral for student success, as this allows students to be more efficient, diligent, and comprehensive, as they are planning, organized, structured, and completing tasks before they are due. Poor time and stress management lead to irritability, exhaustion, difficulty focusing, forgetfulness, and depression. Therefore, it is vital for educators to help students effectively manage time and stress so that they feel a sense of accomplishment, relief, and are productive. Some strategies for time and stress management include

- Making a schedule
- Having to-do lists
- Prioritizing tasks in order to accomplish the most important things first
- Deep breathing/meditation
- Using a stress ball to decompress
- Completing assignments before the due date

Time and stress management skills are important for reducing bullying and violence, as these skills help students to be more efficient, engage in self-care, focus, and reduce feelings of frustration, sadness, and anger, allowing them to better perform and cope.

Growth Mindset: Carol Dweck has brought the growth mindset to life in her research and addresses that when students believe they can get smarter they understand that effort makes them stronger and put more time in to their work, leading to higher achievement. The growth mindset emphasizes that learning is not fixed and it can be amplified if given the opportunity and resources to do so. Mindset is important, as it directly impacts the attainment of goals. Dweck found that people who believed in their own intelligence, were more motivated, put in more effort, and were more open to approaching challenges. These people were also more likely to learn from challenges and persevere despite obstacles

(Mindset Works, 2017). Having a growth mindset is instrumental in student performance because when students believe that they can achieve they will be more likely to take steps to do so. Educators MUST emphasize that skills can be amplified and improved if given opportunity, time, and practice. Students who believe in themselves and their abilities are less likely to engage in bullying and violence, as they are focused on working toward self-actualization and becoming the best version of themselves because the possibilities are endless and they realize that they can achieve everything they want to with hard work and effort.

Optimism: Being hopeful, seeing things through a more positive lens, being able to learn from teachable moments; what happened and how this can promote growth moving forward, being hopeful for the future (Umoh, 2017). People who are more optimistic are more positive, have more gratitude, and work hard to be the best they can be (Umoh, 2017). Students who are optimistic are more driven, motivated, compassionate, grateful, and hopeful about the future, which in turn reduces bullying and violence in the school setting.

Leadership: Acting as a leader and role model, being able to delegate tasks, to motivate oneself and others, and to be able to visualize goals and take steps to achieve them. Leadership is critical for school success, as well as success in the workplace, as people must take initiative and work intentionally to achieve goals in order to maximize efficiency. Leadership is vital for students, as it helps them to learn core skills needed to be successful in school and life, as well as the importance of taking steps in order to facilitate positive change. Effective leaders possess strong interpersonal skills, they are effective listeners, have effective time management skills, engage in goal setting, and are accountable. In addition to being goal-oriented, leaders are honest, hardworking, willing to help others, are positive, and responsible (Fulton, 2019). Leaders also are able to motivate others to achieve their goals. According to Fulton (2019), in order to teach leadership skills to students:

- Demonstrate honesty, authenticity, and integrity
- Work hard and persevere in order to overcome challenges
- Communicate effectively
- Make healthy choices
- Think positively and be optimistic
- Demonstrate responsibility

Students with leadership qualities are less likely to engage in bullying or school violence, as they are other-oriented, motivated, diligent, think about the outcome of their actions, are hopeful for the future, and display accountability. Therefore, in order to create safe school climates, giving students leadership roles and opportunities to enhance their leadership is critical.

Creativity: Creativity involves being innovative and being able to take an outside approach in order to problem-solve in a unique way. The partnership for 21st-century skills emphasizes the importance of creativity in order to foster student success and career readiness. Students are encouraged to envision their dreams and augment their creative skills. Creativity entails capturing new ideas, challenging ourselves and solving problems, broadening and boosting creativity by learning about new topics, and surrounding ourselves with diverse people and things (Henderson, 2008). Educators can help students enhance their creativity by:

- Tapping into their imagination
- Giving options when completing tasks
- Making mistakes meaningful and problem-solving using innovative strategies

Enhancing creativity is vital for student success, as well as for reducing bullying and violence, as this allows students to express themselves rather than internalizing emotions, gives students power, allows students to explore and integrate their strengths into their work, and fosters authenticity and transparency. Creativity helps to foster acceptance, celebration, inclusion, unity, and ingenuity, which are all integral for developing safe and uplifting school climates.

Resilience: Resilience is a critical skill to possess. We all face challenges in life. It is vital for students to learn to become resilient so that they do not allow challenges to impede their growth. Educators must encourage students to persevere despite obstacles in order to achieve their goals and dreams. There is only one direction—moving forward. Students who are resilient are more likely to achieve, as they continue working diligently in order to overcome struggles. Resilience is vital, as this helps students to tap into their intrinsic motivation to move forward and overcome hardships. According to Brooke's Publishing (2017), in order to enhance resilience in students' educators can

- Encourage students to develop a sense of responsibility.
- Increase students' sense of ownership by allowing them to solve problems themselves and giving them decision-making opportunities.
- Help students to establish self-discipline and control, have students help develop classroom rules and consequences, as this will enable students to better follow them.
- Promote self-advocacy skills to stand up for their values and beliefs.
- Provide positive feedback and encouragement. Students appreciate having emotional support and encouragement. Focusing on students' positives and accomplishments is a helpful way to boost resilience.
- Teaching students to cope with mistakes and failure, as this is a part of life. The importance here is learning from mistakes rather than

being defined by them and determining what to do differently in the future in order to have more positive outcomes.

Resilience is critical for helping to mitigate bullying and violence in that students who are resilient are able to bounce back and do not allow challenges to impede their growth; they rise above and move forward. Resilience is also important, as many perpetrators carrying out acts of violence experience feelings of rage, sadness, loneliness, and hopelessness. Therefore, teaching students to be resilient will help them to become stronger, braver, more self-aware, and better able to cope with challenges in a healthy and constructive manner.

Grit: Having passion about working toward achieving goals. Grit is a quality that enables people to work diligently and follow-through on their long-term passions and goals. Students who possess grit are more driven, dedicated, and demonstrate greater tenacity in school and life. The more challenging things that students can accomplish, the more that students know that they are capable of doing challenging tasks. Grit is one's ability to overcome challenges, bounce back, and learn from failure. According to Shirk (2020), educators can help students to enhance grit by:

- Identifying passions
- Giving students challenging tasks, as the more challenging things they do, the more that they believe in their abilities to overcome challenges.
- Learning not to quit and to continue working toward achieving long-term goals.
- Letting kids struggle. This is important, as we cannot always save them and jump in. Through sadness or frustration, students can develop resilience by going outside of their comfort zone.
- Celebrating failure and mistakes, as this is how learning and growth take place.

Grit is important for overcoming bullying and violence, in that students who have grit cope with losses, sadness, anger, and frustration in constructive ways. Rather than lashing out physically, they are able to manage their emotions and use their emotions to push them forward in a positive direction. Students with grit are able to deal with loss, as they realize it is a part of life and continue working toward bettering themselves and achieving goals. Thus, helping all students to enhance grit is critical for a safe and engaging school climate.

Character: Character dictates how we think feel and act and it reflects skills and values that enable people to display respect and responsibility (Jones et al., 2017). The character embodies hardworking, diligence, tenacity, self-control, and self-efficacy (Lickona & Davidson, 2005). Character helps to foster ethical behavior, as well as goal achievement, strength, and resilience. Character is important for dealing with bullying and reducing violence in schools, as students who possess strong character to demonstrate responsibility for self and others, respect, citizenship, fairness, and justice for all. Implementing character education programs in elementary school are paramount, as programs such as Learning for Life and Character Counts teach students about the core character traits and the importance of possessing them in order to be successful in school and life. The earlier students can learn and execute these traits, the more successful they will be.

Interpersonal skills are skills that allow people to interact well with others. Interpersonal skills are skills that are needed to effectively communicate, interact with, and collaborate with others. In order to be successful in school and in the workforce, people must possess strong interpersonal skills to establish meaningful connections, to work effectively and efficiently, to be able to communicate in a transparent way, to be productive, and to be able to work as a team. Interpersonal skills are known as people skills or soft skills and are related to how people communicate and interact. Interpersonal skills include the following:

Communication: Interpersonal communication and our ability to send and receive messages efficiently are vital for school and life success. We must teach students how to actively listen rather than to passively hear. Active listening consists of using appropriate nonverbal communication including body posture, proximity, eye contact, and using minimal encouragers (mm-hmm/uh-huh) to show the person talking that we are understanding what they are saying. Communication is vital for feeling heard, validated, and empowered. We communicate 85% of the time nonverbally and so we have to make sure that students' verbal and nonverbal communication are congruent. According to CASEL (2021), a strong sense of self-awareness can assist in enhancing communication skills.

Conflict resolution: Conflict resolution skills and the ability to negotiate is paramount for students; especially in regard to solving problems in a proactive and peaceful manner. Conflict resolution requires collaboration, active listening, and compromise in order to make sure that both parties involved feel a sense of validation. Conflict resolution involves the **three** R's: recognizing conflict, responding to conflict, and resolving conflict. Students need to be attentive, communicate openly, and be dedicated to collaborating and working together. As educators, we are encouraged to teach students how to identify challenges, understand the interests of those involved, list solutions, assess and select options, and agree to move forward (Hicks, 2021). In order to reduce school violence, students MUST possess effective conflict resolution skills in order to work through issues and decrease the likelihood of revenge and retaliation, which appear to be the leading causes of violence.

Accountability: Accountability is critical for student success. Students must take accountability for their actions rather than deflect or blame others. It is important to experience teachable moments, as people walk away stronger and wiser as a result of going through life experiences. Accountability helps students to take responsibility for their actions and helps to improve behavior and academic achievements. Accountability is extremely important in regard to reducing violence and bullying in schools, as students must be held accountable for their actions, choices, learn from their mistakes, and understand the short and long-term consequences of their choices. Ownership can be modeled and learned. Additionally, it is vital for schools to set rules and expectations so that students understand what is acceptable and what is not acceptable. Rules and expectations need to be consistent; having follow-through and organization is important for student success.

Empathy: Empathy is an integral skill for people to possess, as this goes deeper than compassion. Empathy is about putting ourselves in another person's shoes and taking on their feelings as if they were our own. It is going deeper to understand that person's perspective and to imagine how they feel and how we would feel if in the same situation. Empathy is a key element of emotional intelligence because we are able to understand what others are experiencing as if we are feeling it ourselves. Empathy is key for reducing violence and bullying because before people act a certain way they can imagine that action being done to them and how they would feel and in turn helps to build compassion, cohesion, and inclusion while reducing volatility.

According to Goleman (2021), empathy involves

- Understanding others and sensing others.
- Developing others in regard to acting on the needs and concerns of others and helping them to reach their full potential.
- Having service orientation in regard to putting the needs of others first and looking for ways to help them reach needs/goals.
- Leveraging diversity in terms of being able to create and develop opportunities by collaborating with diverse populations and celebrating similarities and differences.

Positive attitude: Having a positive attitude and mindset is vital for success in school and life. Having a positive attitude allows for enhanced motivation, focus, enjoyment, relaxation, less stress, and welcoming of new experiences. Positive attitudes help students to learn and appreciate being in school. Positivity is a choice and every day we can wake up and choose to be positive. Saying affirmations each day is a wonderful strategy to use to boost positivity. For instance, waking up in the morning and in the mirror saying:

- I am strong
- I am brave

- I am kind
- I am wise
- I can do anything I set my mind to

Saying positive affirmations helps to put us in a positive mindset so no matter what else happens throughout the day, we are able to see things in a more positive light and remain optimistic. Positivity is powerful. It helps to shield against feelings of anxiety and depression, as it wards of sadness and helps people to experience gratitude. When students are happier, they are filled with more joy and peace, leading to enhanced academics, being a better friend, and having a more inclusive and safer school climate (Your Therapy Source, 2019). Positivity has shown to improve health and boost immunity, increase satisfaction in school and life, as we focus on things we are grateful for, it helps us grow and encourages us to take risks, which leads to learning, and also allows us to learn from our mistakes and find the value in them. Having a positive attitude leads to less bullying and violence, because when students are happy, they are more supportive of themselves and others, more focused on their academics, and have a genuine desire for themselves and others to succeed.

Teamwork and collaboration: Research has shown that teaching students how to listen, work together, and ask important questions allows for more learning. Through collaboration, students get to communicate, listen, exchange ideas, make shared decisions, and learn from one another. Rules can be set such as one person talks at a time, all must be respectful, no put-downs in order to remind students of expectations when working collaboratively (Alber, 2017). Collaboration also allows for respect building, as everyone working together must treat one another how they themselves would want to be treated. Further, collaboration promotes accountability, as each student is responsible for a different role when completing an activity. Collaboration allows for enhanced communication, as well as empathy building. Students can use the Three Then Me rule in which the student would have to wait for three others to share before they do (Alber, 2017). Collaboration allows for negotiating, problem-solving, and building mutual respect. Collaboration is KEY for reducing violence in schools, as it fosters togetherness, unity, teamwork, inclusivity, involvement, engagement, and connectivity for all so that students do not feel isolated or excluded; everyone is heard and everyone is important. Students work together as a team to accomplish a common goal.

Conscientiousness: Conscientiousness and having a strong work ethic is monumentally important for student success. Students who are conscientious are more motivated. Those who are conscientious achieve more academically (Conrad & Patry, 2012). Conscientiousness can be enhanced by offering students opportunities to help out, setting rules and consequences, acting as a role model, and providing constructive feedback.

Feedback is critical, as it points out areas of strengths, as well as areas for improvement, which we have to be mindful of, as there is always room for growth. Students who are conscientious do better in school, as they are more focused and attentive. Conscientiousness is one of the broad five domains of personality in the Five-Factor Model of Personality and this is the main model for describing core personality areas (Anderson, 2020). Conscientiousness involves aspects of personalities that reflect the degree to which they are goal-oriented and responsible and work diligently to get things done. It is a skill that can be practiced and improved upon. Conscientiousness positively impacts motivation and persistence, as those that are focused are more motivated and driven to achieve their goals (Anderson, 2020). Agreeableness in regard to one's tendency to cooperate and be empathic and stability in regard to having a calm disposition also relates to conscientiousness, because students who possess these skills work hard, work well with others, and are able to regulate behaviors and remain collected (Anderson, 2020). Being conscientious and hardworking helps to reduce violence in school, as students are focused on achieving, doing their best, supporting others, are tenacious, and driven to reach their fullest potential, rather than tearing others down; when everyone succeeds everyone wins.

Motivation: Motivation is a vital skill for students to possess. Students who lack motivation may struggle with anxiety and depression, due to fear of falling behind, as well as disappointment and sadness that they may be struggling academically. Students who are motivated are more likely to participate and less likely to disrupt. Students who lack motivation may be disengaged or distracted by extraneous variables. Motivated students are more likely to learn and share and have a love of learning. In order to motivate students, educators can encourage them, offer incentives or rewards to work toward achieving a goal and make learning relevant. When students find information to be relevant and applicable to their own lives, this helps to enhance motivation and engagement. Motivation is a critical factor in student success academically, socially, emotionally, and behaviorally, as it is the driving force that enables students to make healthy and constructive choices. Students who lack motivation may feel a lack of connection to school or material, experience emotional problems, or anger. According to the National Board for Professional Teaching Standards (2018), in order to enhance student motivation, educators can do the following:

- Creating an accepting climate.
- Providing directions and feedback.
- Identifying and building upon student strength in order to help them achieve goals.
- Develop course work that is relevant, practical, and relatable to their lives, as that fosters connection and engagement.

- Encourage parental involvement.
- Use positive reinforcement such as verbal praise or a reward system.
- Help boost students' self-esteem, as the better students feel about themselves and the more confident they are in their abilities, the more motivated they will be to achieve excellence.
- Promoting a growth mindset over a fixed mindset. Teach students that skills are learned and enhanced via time and practice. Many students may not partake in challenges because they do not want to make mistakes or struggle. However, by helping to foster a growth mindset, this will help the student to recognize that their skills and talents can be improved through effort.
- Developing a meaningful relationship with students is vital for motivation. We must believe in them in order for them to believe in themselves. Getting to know students and their passions, allows educators to integrate students' interests into learning, making it more relevant.
- Establishing high expectations and clear goals is vital for motivation, as this lets students know what is expected. Having transparency is key. Setting up daily learning goals can be helpful in order to keep students focused and on track. Setting high expectations for learning and behavior is also integral for critical thinking and learning.
- Being inspirational is key for motivation. Educators can share their successes in order to motivate their students to achieve greatness through perseverance and hard work.

Motivation is important for reducing bullying and school violence, as students are driven to succeed academically, behaviorally, and emotionally, they feel supported and encouraged, and students who are motivated thrive in climates that are peaceful, rigorous, accepting, cohesive, collaborative, celebratory, and uplifting.

References

Alber, R. (2017). *Deeper learning: A collaborative classroom is key*. Retrieved from https://www.edutopia.org/blog/deeper-learning-collaboration-key-rebecca-alber

American School Counselor Association (2012). *The ASCA national model: A framework for school counseling programs* (3rd ed.). Alexandria, VA: ASCA.

American School Counselor Association (2019). *The ASCA national model: A framework for school counseling programs* (4th ed.). Alexandria, VA: ASCA.

Anderson, S. C. (2020). *Conscientious children do better in school*. Retrieved from https://www.spsp.org/news-center/blog/calmar-andersen-conscientious-children-school-performance

Berg, J., Osher, D., Moroney, D., & Yoder, N. (2017). *The intersection of school climate and social emotional development*. Retrieved from https://www.air.org/resource/intersection-school-climate-andsocial-and-emotional-development

Brookes Publishing. (2017). *7 ways to foster self-esteem and resilience in all learners*. Retrieved from https://blog.brookespublishing.com/7-ways-to-foster-self-esteem-and-resilience-in-all-learners/

Collaborative for Academic, Social, and Emotional Learning (CASEL) (2021). *What is SEL?* Retrieved from https://casel.org/what-is-SEL/

Conrad, N., & Patry, M. (2012). Conscientiousness and academic performance: A mediational analysis. *International Journal for Scholarship of Teaching and Learning, 6*, 1–16.

Durlak, J. A., Weissberg, R. P., Dymnicki, A. B., Taylor, R. D., & Schellinger, K. B. (2011). The impact of enhancing students' social and emotional learning: A meta-analysis of school-based universal interventions. *Child Development, 82*(1), 405–432. Retrieved from http://casel.org/wp-content/uploads/Meta-Analysis-Child-Development-Full-Article1.pdf

Fried, L. (2011). *Teaching teachers about emotion regulation in the classroom*. Retrieved from https://ro.ecu.edu.au/ajte/vol36/iss3/1/

Fulton, J. (2019). *How to teach leadership skills to your students*. Retrieved from https://www.classcraft.com/blog/how-to-teach-leadership-skills-to-your-students/

Goleman, D. (2021). *What is empathy?* Retrieved from https://www.skillsyouneed.com/ips/empathy.html

Hamre, B. K., & Pianta, R. C. (2007). Learning opportunities in preschool and early elementary classrooms. In R. Pianta, M. Cox, & K. Snow (Eds.), *School readiness & the transition into kindergarten in the era of accountability* (pp. 49–84). Baltimore: Brookes.

Healthline (2021). What you need to know about emotional intelligence. Retrieved from https://www.healthline.com/health/emotional-intelligence#what-is-it

Henderson, J. (2008). Developing students' creative skills for 21st century success. Retrieved from http://www1.ascd.org/publications/newsletters/education-update/dec08/vol50/num12/Developing-Students'-Creative-Skills-for-21st-Century-Success.aspx

Hicks, T. (2021). *Seven steps for effective problem solving in the workplace*. Retrieved from https://www.mediate.com/articles/thicks.cfm

Jones, S., Brush, K., Bailey, R., Brion-Meisels, G., McIntyre, J., Kahn, J., Nelson, B., & Stickle, L. (2017). *Navigating SEL from the inside out. Looking inside and across 25 leading SEL programs: A practical resource for schools and OST providers*. Retrieved from https://www.wallacefoundation.org/knowledge-center/Documents/Navigating-Social-and-Emotional-Learning-from-the-Inside-Out.pdf

Lickona, T., & Davidson, M. (2005). *Smart & good high schools: Integrating excellence and ethics for success in school, work, and beyond*. Cortland, NY: Center for the 4th and 5th RS.

McGraw Hill (2017). 5 guiding principles of social emotional learning. Retrieved from https://medium.com/inspired-ideas-prek-12/5-guiding-principles-of-social-emotional-learning-2f9fb554edad

Mindset Works (2017). *The impact of a growth mindset*. Retrieved from https://www.mindsetworks.com/science/Impact

National Board For Professional Teaching Standards (2018). *Top 5 strategies for motivating students*. Retrieved from https://www.nbpts.org/top-5-strategies-for-motivating-students/

National School Climate Center (2012). *School climate research summary.* Retrieved from https://files.eric.ed.gov/fulltext/ED573683.pdf

Osher, D., Cantor, P., Berg, J., Rose, T., & Steyer, L. (2017). *The Science of learning and development.* Washington, DC: American Institutes for Research, Turnaround for Children, The Opportunity Institute, The Learning Policy Institutes, Education Counsel.

Shirk, T. (2020). *What is grit, why is it important, and how can we develop it?* Retrieved from https://www.schoolrubric.com/what-is-grit-why-is-it-important-how-can-we-develop-it/

Umoh, R. (2017). *Why you should be highly optimistic if you want to be successful.* Retrieved from https://www.cnbc.com/2017/10/05/why-should-you-be-highly-optimistic-if-you-want-to-besuccessful.html.

We Are Teachers (2018). *10 tips for teaching emotional regulation and improving classroom behavior at the same time.* Retrieved from https://www.weareteachers.com/emotional-regulation/

Your Therapy Source (2019). *Importance of a positive attitude for students. Retrieved from* https://www.yourtherapysource.com/blog1/2019/02/26/the-benefits-of-positive-attitudes-in-students/#:~:text=Learn%20from%20your%20mistakes.&text=Students%20who%20learn%20from%20their,share%20those%20experiences%20as%20well

12 Significance of Social Emotional Learning

Significance of Social Emotional Learning

Social Emotional Learning has been shown to increase:

- Students' performance
- Enhance motivation
- Increase self-concept
- Enhance self-sufficiency
- Improve peer relationships
- Increase self-regulation and reduce impulsivity
- Social emotional learning (SEL) is composed of five competencies including self-awareness, self-management, social awareness, relationship skills, and responsible decision-making

Integrating SEL is paramount for student success academically, behaviorally, socially emotionally, and vocationally. Research has substantiated that SEL competencies can be taught, modeled, practiced, and promote positive student outcomes that are integral for success in school and post-graduation (CASEL, 2021). SEL has shown to improve students' skills, attitudes, interpersonal relationships, academic prowess, and overall perceptions of the classroom and school; seeing things more positively. Additionally, SEL has shown to mitigate anxiety, depression, behavioral issues, and substance usage. Furthermore, SEL has led to longer-term improvements in students' skills, attitudes, prosocial and constructive behavior, and academic performance all necessary for success in the school and workforce.

Society at large and schools today are so incredibly diverse with students from a variety of backgrounds. Therefore, integration SEL into curricula is fundamentally important, as it has been shown to help create a safe school climate, promote positivity, and augment students' success in school, as well as in post-secondary endeavors. According to Weissberg (2016), in addition to SEL improving achievement by 11 percentile

DOI: 10.4324/9781003262183-12

points, it also has shown to promote prosocial behaviors including responsibility, respect, kindness, compassion, empathy, improves student perceptions about the school, as well as mitigates student depression and stress (Durlak et al., 2011). SEL emphasizes the importance of its five core competencies (Weissberg, 2016):

- Self-awareness and understanding emotions, goals, and values, as well as identifying strengths and areas for improvement.
- Self-management and regulating emotions and behaviors in regard to delaying gratification, being disciplined, being in control of impulses, and being proactive rather than reactive.
- Social awareness in regard to understanding, learning, empathizing with, celebrating diversity, and displaying compassion for others.
- Relationship skills in regard to maintaining and building healthy relationships, listening, resolving conflict peacefully, and offering help when needed.
- Responsible decision-making in regard to making healthy choices and constructive choices about behavior and social interactions.

Furthermore, SEL programs should be comprised of four elements that reflect the acronym SAFE (Durlak et al., 2011), including

- Sequenced and connected in order to promote skill development
- Active in regard to having experiential forms of learning to foster growth
- Focused in order to emphasize personal and social skills
- Explicit: Focusing on specific SEL skills to enhance

Students who possess SEL skills are more driven, demonstrate more self-control, are able to engage in perspective sharing, possess more positive attitudes about school, build healthier relationships with peers and faculty, experience fewer disciplinary issues, and have higher grades, GPA, and test scores, and make healthy choices that benefit themselves and others (Durlak et al., 2011). Enhanced SEL skills have been shown to improve graduation rates, boost career readiness, augment relationships and interpersonal skills, enhance mental health and wellness, as well as reduce at-risk behavior (Durlak et al., 2011). Research has shown that having a safe school climate promotes both academic performances and the mental health wellness of students (Thapa, Cohen, Gulley, & Higgins-D'Alessandro, 2013). School administrators, counselors, and educators play an instrumental role in implementing school-wide activities that help to create a positive school climate. Integrating anti-bullying programs and policies are key in order to increase school climates. As noted by Weissberg (2016), integrating SEL effectively requires using a multi-tiered approach by all critical stakeholders in order to make sure that all students are reaping the rewards. SEL skills can be integrated into school-wide programs, classroom instruction, small groups, and individual settings.

Some researchers say that being able to demonstrate empathy, asking for help, goal setting, motivation, collaboration, and ability to problem-solve helps students in school and life and maybe even **more** important than academic abilities (Garcia, 2021). There is truth to this in that you can have a student who has straight A's and perfect test scores, but if that student lacks emotional intelligence and has difficulty communicating, problem-solving, demonstrating self-control, and lacks optimism, that student despite their intellect, will likely struggle in the workforce. Students who lack SEL skills are more likely to struggle when dealing with conflict, coping, dealing with stress, behavior, social skills, and communication. In a study conducted by Bridgeland, Dilulio, and Morison (2006), the researchers found that 70% of students who dropout do so because they may lack the SEL skills to overcome challenges faced in school. It has been shown that SEL skills improve academic outcomes and classroom behaviors for students (Garcia, 2021). The five core competencies including self-awareness, self-management, relationship skills, social awareness, and responsible decision-making can be taught.

In regard to enhancing self-management, educators can

- Model self-management
- Encourage goal setting
- Acknowledge students who are on task
- Give leadership roles

In regard to increasing social awareness, educators can

- Create an atmosphere celebrating diversity
- Encourage sharing and discourse so that students can listen to one another's perspectives, as that fosters growth

In regard to amplifying responsible decision-making educators can:

- Work with students on helping them to make healthy choices
- Give students vignettes to problem-solve and ask them to weigh the pros and cons of their choices

In regard to enhancing relationship skills, educators can

- Use small groups
- Have students role-play scenarios focusing on problem-solving
- Address the importance of communication and active listening

In regard to boosting self-awareness, educators can

* Name skills they are using
* Use small groups to enhance collaboration
* Identify areas of strength, as well as areas that necessitate growth

Each of these competencies is significant to build and enhance, as they have each shown to augment reflective practice, self-control, strength, courage, communication and interpersonal relationships, acceptance, inclusivity, problem-solving, coping skills, accountability, and empathy; all instrumental for increasing student success and decreasing school violence.

Moreover, due to the pandemic, educators and parents are trying to find ways to instill SEL skills in their students and children. SEL is now considered to be one of the most integral aspects of impactful education (The Write Of Your Life, 2020), as it provides a core foundation for learning outcomes, as well as college and career readiness. Schools that implement SEL have more peaceful school settings in which ALL students are excelling. SEL is pivotal as it addresses how students can engage and connect to others through respect, understanding, empathy, and validation. SEL also provides students with a healthy self-concept, as well as helps to mitigate feelings of sadness, depression, and stress (The Write Of Your Life, 2020). In addition to students who receive SEL training that enhance their GPA by 11%, SEL also has shown to mitigate dropout rates by approximately 12%, as well as reduced disciplinary issues. Physical aggression and fights in school also were reduced by approximately 42% (The Write Of Your Life, 2020). Furthermore, SEL has shown to mitigate substance usage, teen pregnancy, and delinquent behaviors therefore helping students to be proactive, to more effectively problem-solve, to be intentional, thoughtful, and helping them to make informed decisions. Due to its influential impact, educators universally are encouraged to integrate SEL into their curricula; especially school counselors, as they are trained professionals who specialize in supporting the whole student.

In regard to integrating SEL:

* Stakeholders can start their day by asking students to check in and allow students to process their emotions prior to addressing content, as this will allow for expression, communication, sharing, disclosure, conversation, and student feelings of importance and acceptance (Write of Your Life, 2020).
* Further, rather than utilizing punitive punishment for students, as that tends to exacerbate an issue, educators are encouraged to discuss the issue, address the importance of empathy, compassion, effective problem-solving, and emotion regulation, as that will help the

student to identify more positive ways to react in the future; making it a teachable moment.
*   Having students work in small groups is another impactful way to incorporate SEL into instruction, as this enables discussion, problem-solving, building social skills, effective problem-solving, open-mindedness, and collaboration; all critical life skills (Write of Your Life, 2020).

Additionally, SEL has shown to be an effective financial investment according to cost-benefit research in that for every dollar invested there is a fiscal return of 11 dollars. Thus, more money invested into SEL will lead to a more competitive economy and more financial success holistically (Pennsylvania State University, 2017). In order to augment our K12 school systems to ensure that all students are learning and mastering SEL skills, we must focus on prompting equity for all. SEL focuses on education, the workforce, relationship building, collaboration, developing culturally responsive climates, providing students with leadership roles, building resilience, as well as helping them to problem-solve more proactively. By implementing SEL students can enhance their academic performance, social skills, be more well-adjusted, better able to cope, and be more prepared for the competitive workforce upon graduation.

SEL and Enhancing College and Career Readiness

SEL plays an instrumental role in college and career readiness, as it provides students with knowledge regarding fundamental skills including collaboration, emotion regulation, time/stress management, problem-solving, diversity, motivation, zest, optimism, leadership, and accountability in order to be successful in K-12, as well as in their post-secondary endeavors. In addition to the importance of academic success, students must possess SEL skills in order to achieve success in college or the workforce. Businesses and employers want their employees to be intuitive and responsive. Today, collaboration and relationship building are required at work and in society at large (Committee for Children, 2018). Students gain 13% point gain in academic achievement when exposed to SEL (Gulbrandson, 2019). Additionally, dropout rates, behavioral issues, mental health struggles, as well as at-risk behavior decrease when students possess SEL skills, as they are more resilient, able to overcome adversity, are motivated and persevere until they achieve their goals (Gulbrandson, 2019). Students who possess a high degree of self-awareness (aware of the impact on others), self-management (ability to regulate emotions), relationship skills (ability to build healthy relationships), social awareness (celebrate diversity and are open-minded), as well as responsible decision-making skills (making healthy choices), are more likely to be successful in school and in life (Gulbrandson, 2019). In addition to every dollar invested in SEL which leads to a fiscal return of 11 dollars, the more money that is invested into SEL leads to having a more fiscally competitive economy and success worldwide (Gulbrandson, 2019). In order to ensure student success for all, counselors and educators must focus on integrating SEL into their curricula. SEL helps to amplify education, employment, relationships, collaboration, leadership, empathy, culturally responsive school climates, and gives students the opportunity to enhance their conflict resolution and problem-solving skills; critical for college and career success. Through integrating SEL practices and policies, students nationwide will be more competent, prepared, and capable of making positive contributions to the workforce.

There are core SEL skills that are advantageous for children and teenagers to possess in order to be college and career ready including:

- **Cognitive Regulation:** Basic skill need for goal achievement in that it allows students to prioritize their behavior and allows for students to engage in prosocial behaviors. Cognitive regulation allows for health decision-making and problem-solving (Diamond & Lee, 2011). This teaches students to think about what they are saying prior to it being said. Cognitive regulation entails control memory and flexibility which are all needed to enhance career readiness (Jones et al., 2017).
- **Emotional Processes:** Emotion regulation helps students to identify and regulate their emotions, as well as become more aware of the feelings of others (Jones et al., 2017). This skill helps students to become less impulsive, have greater self-restraint and control. Having emotion regulation helps to increase self-awareness, friendship building, perspective-taking, and problem-solving; all critical for career readiness, as people must be able to work together, share their ideas, be respectful, and get the job done regardless of differences they may have. Problem-solving and impulse control allow people to resolve problems peacefully, be methodical, and think before acting. Students must learn emotion regulation skills so that they can be intentional, organized, prepared, and collected; all vital for improving productivity at work (Jones et al., 2017).
- **Social and Interpersonal Skills:** Allow students to share ideas, perspectives, improve communication, talk, express, and interact more effectively with peers and future colleagues. Social and interpersonal skills are essential for unity, teamwork, collaboration, problem-solving, and being able to work well with others. People may have different mindsets and approaches, but the job needs to get done efficiently and correctly and that requires collaboration and negotiation. It is important for people to be able to work through problems and solve them collaboratively while communicating in an open manner, as this helps to validate, foster understanding, and increase productivity in school and in the workforce (Jones et al., 2017).

SEL skills act as a template for instruction, as they showcase the goals and benchmarks needed for each student to reach in regard to what they should be able to accomplish. Learning standards identify the competencies that students need to work to achieve so that they have the ability to reach their fullest potential (CASEL, 2021). Learning standards allow stakeholders to create a climate that fosters SEL and the intrapersonal and interpersonal communication skills needed in order to attain academic, personal/social, emotional, and vocational success. Peart (2019) indicated that SEL is integral for career success in that those who are motivated to learn, are resilient and display flexibility, are collaborative, have effective communication skills, are empathic, and creative are more productive in the workplace (Peart, 2019). In order to help employees reach their potential, they need to be able to manage their emotions, be mindful, grounded, and centered, be able to stay in the present, have effective communication skills, demonstrate resilience and work to overcome adversity to be stronger and wiser as a result of dealing with challenges (Stahl, 2018). SEL must be integrated into curricula in order to foster a positive school climate that maximizes academic, social, emotional, behavioral, and vocational success for all.

There is plentiful research validating the positive impact SEL has on both academic and workplace success. Social and emotional learning is comprised of a comprehensive framework that emphasizes the important SEL skills necessary for all students to experience academic, social/emotional, and vocational success. The Committee for Children (2018) and CASEL (2021) have both substantiated that students who are knowledgeable, able to build healthy relationships, regulate their emotions, are empathic, can collaborate and communicate, are able to manage time and stress, can actively listen, appreciate diversity, and problem-solve effectively experience enhanced job performance and success in the workplace. SEL fervently supports the pillars of academic achievement in regard to teamwork, problem-solving, empathy, and relatability, which are paramount for formulating relationships in the workforce. Relationship building is an integral aspect of SEL as this allows us to be more collaborative and work in a team setting, which is imperative for school and workplace success. In today's global society, people work as a team rather than in isolation in order to complete tasks effectively. Companies that thrive, have employees who are emotionally intelligent, communicative, intuitive, have zest, and intrinsic motivation to work toward their fullest potential (Committee for Children, 2018). Thus, it is imperative for PK-12 schools to incorporate SEL into their curricula. Counselors are encouraged to collaborate with teachers on integrating SEL into lessons and curricula in order to address stress management, emotion regulation, anger management, conflict resolution, communication, collaboration, diversity, leadership, and accountability.

Creating a school climate that is career-ready also helps to mitigate bullying and school violence, as students are organized, structured, motivated to learn, collaborative, inclusive, supportive, unified, passionate, and hyper-focused on working toward achieving similar goals; their success and the success of their peers. Therefore, in order to develop peaceful school climates and school climates that are challenging and preparatory, stakeholders must ensure that students are equipped with the necessary knowledge and SEL skills needed in order to be successful in today's competitive and ever-changing society.

SEL and Promoting Mental Health

SEL has a direct and positive impact on mental health and wellness. This is especially significant, as many students are struggling with mental health issues that have now been amplified monumentally due to the pandemic. In addition to SEL helping to foster academic success in regard to boosting test scores and GPA, as well as reducing behavioral issues, SEL has also been shown to promote mental health and wellness. Recently, there has been a heavy focus placed on SEL and how it correlates to mental health. SEL is a term used to reflect how a student is able to regulate emotion and to be able to identify that there is a thought that's happening to impact the body and then changing behavior in a way that is either constructive or destructive (Balow, 2018). In contrast, mental health is the outcome of a person's ability to integrate SEL skills learned (Balow, 2018). According to Balow (2018) although there are striking similarities between SEL and mental health there are also clear differences in that there are students with mental health needs that can benefit from SEL, but SEL alone may not be enough to help that student struggling with mental health needs. SEL competencies are taught through a student-centered approach in order to help connect students to the learning process and develop critical thinking, problem-solving, coping, communication, motivation, and emotion regulation skills. SEL has shown to positively impact peer relationships, decision, making, self-awareness, self-management, and social awareness in students both inside and outside of school (Barlow, 2018). It is important to note that SEL does NOT encompass mental health conditions such as PTSD, depression, obsessive-compulsive disorder, or anxiety. SEL has shown to positively impact students struggling with ADHD and intermittent explosive disorder (Barlow, 2018). It is also important to note that although SEL skills cannot take away symptoms associated with mental health issues, possessing SEL skills can help students better cope if they are struggling with a mental health disorder, as it provides students with resources and tools to overcome life challenges.

As mental health is at the forefront, integrating SEL into curricula is vital. 13–20% of students living in the United States are impacted by mental health disorders; approximately 10 million students. In other words, a school with 500 students may have 100 students who are struggling with mental health issues (Barlow, 2018). Typically, students may struggle with mood disorders, anxiety, depression, or bipolar disorder, as well as attention deficit hyperactivity disorder (ADHD) (Barlow, 2018). Furthermore, suicide rates which can be augmented by mental health-related concerns are the second leading cause of death amongst students 12–17 years old. Mental health issues that are left untreated impact students academically, socially, behaviorally, psychologically, and emotionally. Students who are struggling with untreated mental health issues may have difficulty in school with following directions, focusing, resolving conflicts, remaining engaged, and may lack self-control (Barlow, 2018). Students who may have trouble controlling emotions and building friendships can experience feelings of disengagement and disconnectedness, further highlighting the relationship between SEL and mental health. Students who feel isolated, alone, sad, lack friendships, are struggling with depression or anxiety, may avoid school, experience bullying, or be more at risk for carrying out acts of violence, as they may lack a support system, are struggling with their mental health, lack coping skills, and struggle with impulsivity. Mental health illnesses that are undiagnosed can lead to aggression, bullying, self-injury, substance abuse (Barlow, 2018), suicide, or homicide. Thus, it is pivotal and schools focus on the needs of the whole child by addressing mental health, as well as SEL, as even though they are separate entities, they are both very much interrelated.

Moreover, in 1999, the US Surgeon General defined mental health as successful functioning that allows for productive activities, fulfilling relationships with others, and the ability to adapt to change and to cope with adversity (Mental Health: A Report of the Surgeon General, 1999). This report demonstrated the importance of emphasizing mental health in school, promoted the importance of family involvement, as well as showed the importance of addressing social, emotional, and behavioral challenges (Collaborative for Academic, Social, and Emotional Learning, 2008). Research has shown that universal mental health supports positively impact child and adolescent development. More than half of all lifetime cases of mental health disorders start at age 14. Schools can play a role in helping students address mental health issues, as there are numerous supports in schools for students who are at risk of struggling with a mental health disorder. Schools have the ability to impact a large number of students and can promote universal mental health (Collaborative for Academic, Social, and Emotional Learning, 2008). It has been established that although schools are primarily focused on academic achievement, mental health and social emotional development are integral for learning. According to Collaborative for Academic, Social, and Emotional Learning (2008), the promotion of SEL in schools further supports mental health through teaching-related skills that foster the holistic success of students.

In accordance with Collaborative for Academic, Social, and Emotional Learning (2008) in order to foster the mental health of ALL students, schools are encouraged to:

- Integrate resources and create interventions that foster healthy development.
- Provide mental health resources.
- Facilitate responsive services (school counselors can conduct individual, small group, and classroom counseling) sessions on a myriad of topics related to SEL and mental health.
- Encourage early intervention to provide resources early on and to identify students who are struggling prior to issues escalating.
- Provide help to those with severe struggles.
- Increase protective factors such as supportive relationships between peers and faculty.
- Create safe and caring school climates.
- Take a student-centered approach.
- Encourage collaboration with families, as well as outside agencies in order to provide additional support for struggling students.

Moreover, SEL teaches students skills to be successful in school and in life. These skills are pivotal for all students and can be especially helpful for students struggling with mental health issues. SEL reinforces how to enhance self-control, build relationships, develop care and concern for others, make healthy choices, and handle adversity in a healthy way. SEL can help to teach students how to self-soothe and to de-escalate when feeling angry, as well as how to impactfully solve conflicts. SEL teaches students the skills necessary to be engaged learners and to have healthy relationships with peers and faculty (Collaborative for Academic, Social, and Emotional Learning, 2008), which is vital for academic performance, improved behaviors, decreased bullying, and school violence. SEL can help to augment students' mental health by helping schools emphasize skill development, as well as creating a safe and nurturing environment for ALL students to thrive (Collaborative for Academic, Social, and Emotional Learning, 2008).

Collaborative for Academic, Social, and Emotional Learning (2008) states that SEL programs may reduce the number of students who need early intervention because SEL programs help to provide skills that students need to deal with challenges, as well as helps teachers to promote connectivity and engagement. For students who may require more support, SEL skills can be further incorporated into mental health interventions. SEL helps students to become more compassionate and supportive, further helping to reduce bullying and school violence. Although SEL does not replace mental health services for students who are struggling with a mental health disorder, it does help to provide a framework that allows for early intervention for struggling students. SEL also teaches necessary skills to deal with challenges and to help struggling students to better cope, as well as fosters student academic, social, emotional, psychological, vocational, and life success.

There are some schools today that are making SEL a mandatory part of their curricula and these schools appear to have a better understanding of their students' needs and well-being, as well as work intentionally to create a positive climate for their students and staff. In addition to emphasizing core subjects such as Math, Science, and English, schools are also prioritizing SEL and integrating some of these strategies to do so:

- Integrating advisory allows students to process their mental health and connect with faculty and peers (Tierney, 2020).
- Empower students to lead and help others make positive decisions, as this helps to strengthen peer influence and create a more positive school culture (Tierney, 2020).
- Restorative justice circles for students to process challenges they are facing, as well as to enhance inclusion, disclosure, normalization, and collaboration.
- Promoting high academic standards.
- Promoting accountability and ensuring that faculty and students model healthy behavior and follow school protocol.
- Assign peer buddies to each student who can watch out for that student so if something alarming happens, stakeholders can be notified and proper supports can be put in place.
- Providing professional development and support for faculty (Collaborative for Academic, Social, and Emotional Learning, 2008).
- Create calm down area for students that encourages deep breathing and self-soothing in order to enhance self-regulation.
- Integrate meditation and mindfulness each day in order to help students become more grounded and centered.
- Provide specific feedback.
- Utilize small group and cooperative learning.
- Incorporating anti-bullying programs such as No Place for Hate and Steps to Respect.
- Integrating SEL competencies (self-awareness/self-management/relationship skills/social awareness/decision-making and intrapersonal/interpersonal skills) into curricula.
- School counselors facilitate individual, small group, and classroom counseling addressing SEL topics.
- Conduct workshops for faculty and parents on SEL and ways to augment SEL skills.

There are a variety of ways in which schools can help to teach and reinforce SEL in order to improve the academic and mental health and wellness of students. SEL is advantageous for ALL students in regard to fostering personal and professional growth; including those struggling with mental health disorders. SEL and mental health can be addressed in conjunction with one another, as both strive to help people reach their fullest potential. Although SEL cannot be used in lieu of mental health interventions, the skills and principles learned can certainly supplement, complement, and further promote mental health and wellness.

References

Barlow, C. (2018). Social emotional learning vs. mental health: What is the difference? Retrieved from https://www.illuminateed.com/blog/2018/10/social-emotional-learning-vs-mental-health-whats-the-difference/

Bridgeland, J., Dilulio, J., & Morison, K. (2006). *The silent epidemic: Perspectives of high school dropouts.* Retrieved from https://docs.gatesfoundation.org/documents/thesilentepidemic3-06final.pdf

Collaborative for Academic, Social, and Emotional Learning (CASEL) 2008). *Connecting social emotional learning with mental health.* Retrieved from https://files.eric.ed.gov/fulltext/ED505361.pdf

Collaborative for Academic, Social, and Emotional Learning (CASEL) (2021). *What is SEL?* Retrieved from https://casel.org/fundamentals-of-sel/

Committee for Children (2018). *How SEL allows children to succeed in school, the workplace, and in life.* Retrieved from https://www.cfchildren.org/blog/2018/05/how-sel-helps-kids-succeed/

Diamond, A., & Lee, K. (2011). Interventions shown to aid executive function development in children 4 to 12 years old. *Science, 33*, 959–964.

Durlak, J. A., Weissberg, R. P., Dymnicki, A. B., Taylor, R. D., & Schellinger, K. B. (2011). The impact of enhancing students' social and emotional learning: A meta-analysis of school-based universal interventions. *Child Development, 82*(1), 405–432. Retrieved from http://casel.org/wp-content/uploads/Meta-Analysis-Child-Development-Full-Article1.pdf

Garcia, S. (2021). *How SEL helps you as a teacher.* Retrieved from https://www.understood.org/en/school-learning/for-educators/empathy/how-sel-helps-you-as-a-teacher?utm_source=google&utm_medium=paid&utm_campaign=evr grn-may20-edu&gclid=Cj0KCQjwvYSEBhDjARIsAJMn0liPhucdChCOlWglxClq5yAxfc7WuKd-SPRLmN18drfFn3fbWtwOxqsaAn8SEALw_wcB

Gulbrandson, K. (2019). Trends in social emotional learning: What are the outcomes? Retrieved from https://www.cfchildren.org/blog/2019/06/trends-in-social-emotional-learning-research-what-are-the-outcomes/

Jones, S., Brush, K., Bailey, R., Brion-Meisels, G., McIntyre, J., Kahn, J., Nelson, B., & Stickle, L. (2017). *Navigating SEL from the inside out. Looking inside and across 25 leading SEL programs: A practical resource for schools and OST providers.* Retrieved from https://www.wallacefoundation.org/knowledge-center/Documents/Navigating-Social-and-Emotional- Learning-from- the-Inside-Out.pdf

Mental Health: A Report of the Surgeon General (1999). Center for Mental Health Services National Institute of Mental Health United States. Public Health Service. Office of the Surgeon General. National Institute of Mental Health Mental health: A Report of the Surgeon General. Retrieved from https://profiles.nlm.nih.gov/spotlight/nn/catalog/nlm:nlmuid-101584932X120-doc

Peart, N. (2019). *The 12 most important skills you need to succeed at work.* Retrieved from https://www.forbes.com/sites/nataliapeart/2019/09/10/the-12-most-important-skills-you-need-to-succeed-at-work/?sh=3c4808f71c6a

Pennsylvania State University (2017). Improving social emotional skills in childhood enhances long-term well being and economic outcomes. https://www.prevention.psu.edu/uploads/files/RWJF.EconomicBrief-Final.pdf

Stahl, A. (2018). *5 ways to develop emotional intelligence*. Retrieved from https://www.forbes.com/sites/ashleystahl/2018/05/29/5-ways-to-develop-your-emotional-intelligence/#64021fe96976.

Thapa, A., Cohen, J., Gulley, S., & Higgins-D'Alessandro, A. (2013). A review of school climate research. *Review of Educational Research, 83*(3), 357–385.

Tierney, L. (2020). *Perspective: Mandatory SEL shows students that mental health is just as important as grades*. Retrieved from https://www.ednc.org/perspective-mandatory-sel-shows-students-that-mental-health-is-just-as-important-as-grades/

The Write of Your Life (2020). *What is social emotional learning and why is it so important*. Retrieved from https://thewriteofyourlife.org/what-is-social-emotional-learning/

Weissberg, R. (2016). *Why social and emotional learning is essential for students.* Retrieved from https://www.edutopia.org/blog/why-sel- essential-for-students-weissberg-durlak-domitrovich-gullotta

13 Social Emotional Learning and Reducing School Violence

As we know gun violence in schools has become pervasive due to having a lack of school counselors and mental health professionals in the school setting to work with at-risk students, having a lack of financial resources to hire mental health professionals, ease of access to firearms, lack of extensive background checks, students with undiagnosed mental health issues, students with violent tempers, students who are bullied, angry, or isolated. Many students who have been victims of bullying are looking to retaliate and seek revenge. Additionally, many perpetrators who carry out acts of violence, feel as though they are losing control over their lives and seek to gain control through mass chaos. COVID-19 has amplified the number of students struggling with mental health issues and many have suffered grief and loss. Therefore, it is more vital now more than ever that school counselors and mental health practitioners are able to provide support and identify students who may be struggling in order to be proactive rather than reactive in helping those students who may have the proclivity to carry out acts of violence.

From 2018 to 2019, there were more than 549 school shootings in the United States (Everytown, 2020). Research has shown that more than half of those shootings carried out by minors in primary and secondary settings have obtained a gun from their home (Everytown, 2020). Thus, it is vital that parents make sure that their firearms are stored in a locked place making it impossible for students to gain access. Gun violence decimates students' sense of safety and security (Everytown, 2020). The United States has the highest incidents of gun violence in schools compared to other countries due to gun access and having a lack of mental health services for those in need (Erickson, 2018). In accordance with Statista Research Department (2022), 116 school shootings took place in 2018 and 110 school shootings took place in 2019 in comparison to 44 school shootings in 2017. Therefore, school shootings had doubled between 2017 and 2018. School shootings take place nationwide and impact both urban and rural schools and impact students of all backgrounds. No one is immune to gun violence.

DOI: 10.4324/9781003262183-13

There are several warning signs that at-risk students present with including that most school shootings are carried out by males aged 14–17 years old. According to the National School Safety Center (2019), many perpetrators carrying out violence:

- May have anger issues
- May have a temper
- May be cruel to other animals
- May struggle with mental health issues
- May post cryptic messages on social media about harming themselves or others
- Post pictures of weapons or make threats
- May have disciplinary issues
- Have few friends and lack a strong support system
- May lack parental involvement
- May be fascinated with violence
- May be depressed or have suicidal/homicidal thoughts or tendencies

Some at-risk students may be struggling with the oppositional defiant disorder (ODD) or conduct disorder (CD). If ODD is left untreated, it can manifest into a CD. According to the Mayo Clinic, ODD can start during the preschool years and almost always before the teen years. ODD behaviors cause impairment between family, peers, and school (Mayo Clinic, 2018). Symptoms of ODD include

- Arguing and having an irritable mood
- Arguing with adults or those in authority
- Having anger or resentment
- Refusing to comply with rules
- Deliberately annoying others
- Lacking accountability and blaming others for choices
- Vindictiveness or revenge

Again, It is important to note that a direct correlation does not exist between mental illness and acts of violence (Kamentz, 2018). However, students who are displaying these warning signs are in need of support and assistance, and providing that early on can help mitigate the propensity for gun violence in schools. One in five students struggle with a mental health illness and four out of five of those students do not receive help. Due to the number of gun tragedies taking place, there is a dire need to have more funds put toward mental health awareness, as well as to hire more mental health practitioners in the schools to counsel and provide assistance to students who display a proclivity for carrying out acts of violence (Teasley, 2018).

Gun violence has a harmful impact on students and stakeholders. The Center for Disease Control and Prevention (2019) has found that an increase in gun violence has taken a massive impact on children and teenagers. Homicide is the second leading cause of death amongst youth aged 5–18 years old. Firearm-related deaths are the second leading cause of death amongst children and teens (Everytown, 2021). Students who witness and experience gun violence are less likely to succeed academically and have lower test scores by approximately 5% (Everytown, 2021) Also known is that test scores in Maths and English are lower (Beland & Kim, 2016). Further, students who experience gun violence have trouble concentrating, experience health issues, are more likely to engage in substance usage, drop out, experience truancy, may have post-traumatic stress disorder, struggle with anxiety or depression, or may display violent tendencies themselves (Everytown, 2021). Many students who experience gun violence may struggle with post-traumatic stress disorder (PTSD), peer issues due to lack of trust issues and inability to form secure attachments (Beland & Kim, 2016). Since safety and order are integral for student learning, measures must be taken to better support all students; specifically, students who may be struggling and displaying warning signs in order to prevent future violence from occurring. Gun violence in schools shatters feelings of safety and protection, and the trepidation, lack of invincibility, and fear that students and faculty experience are unquantifiable. **The million-dollar question seems to be:** What can be done to mitigate gun violence in schools and restore safety and security for all? And the answer is complex. As to this day, there is not a definitive answer. However, we can say with confidence that this is where social emotional learning (SEL) comes to the forefront.

SEL and Reducing School Violence: Prevention Strategies

Due to the pervasiveness of gun violence in schools in the United States, measures must be taken in order to reduce violence, create safer and more secure schools, and most importantly help students to develop into productive, kind, compassionate, and impactful citizens. According to Buchesky (2018), the author notes that gun control is a dead end and due to the divisiveness in the country, it would be advantageous for schools to focus on underlying causes of violence and implement SEL. Although there is no typical profile for a school shooter, there is an ongoing theme for perpetrators in that most of the violence in the schools is committed by students who are struggling with mental health issues (Buchesky, 2018). If violence is to be reduced, mental health needs to be addressed, as well as integrating SEL into curricula. Buchesky (2018) again reiterates that bullying behavior (both being a perpetrator or victim) is strongly correlated with school violence. Antibullying programs are important, as they work to eradicate and raise awareness about the consequences of bullying, but having SEL programs are paramount, as SEL skills help to boost mental health along with relationships. In order to reduce gun violence in schools, schools must work to enhance protective factors such as family involvement, connectedness, positive relationships, conflict re-solution skills, and access to mental health support (Buchesky, 2018). As Buchesky (2018) states, SEL is one of the best tools we have for violence prevention due to its innate ability to focus on relationship building and promoting connectivity along with enhancing academic performance of students. SEL is a type of mental health, as it is helpful for all students and works to destigmatize negative connotations associated with mental health. Through teaching students to express their thoughts and emotions, com-municate their needs, and resolve conflicts verbally and peacefully, this will help to mitigate violence dramatically (Buchesky, 2018).

While working on obtaining their degree, school counselors receive training on the importance of becoming leaders, advocates, and systemic change agents for all students (Young, 2019). School counselors and other key stakeholders including faculty, administrators, parents, and other students play an integral role in identifying students who may have the potential to carry out acts of violence. As the school counselors have a high caseload, consultation and collaboration with other stakeholders are critical in order to identify and provide support to struggling students. Teachers and administrators work with students every day and are mindful of changes in the behavior, academics, and demeanor of their students. Teachers and administrators are encouraged to work with school counselors if they are concerned or believe a student poses a threat to themselves or others so that school counselors are aware of the si-tuation, can involve parents, evaluate the degree of the threat posed, and provide necessary support and resources. Schools are encouraged to have a crisis plan (Studer & Salter, 2010), which outlines protocols to follow in order to ensure safety if a crisis occurs. In addition to having a compre-hensive crisis plan, school counselors must work intentionally to create a school climate that is nurturing, inclusive, empowering, safe, promotes connectivity, is student-centered and rigorous, as these attributes work to motivate, involve, and unify students, as well as help them to experience a sense of belonging; that is critical for student safety and success.

Bullying Prevention

As stated previously, perpetual bullying and seeking revenge/retaliation are the predominant triggers of school violence. SEL emphasizes the importance of empathy, communication, perspective sharing, problem-solving, and accountability. Implementing an antibullying program is a core component of SEL. Therefore, school counselors are encouraged to make students cognizant about the short- and long-term effects of bul-lying, reasons as to why students bully, and the impact of bullying on mental health, self-worth, social skills, suicide, and homicide (Simckes, 2017). The Anti-Defamation League (ADL) created a school-wide antibullying program called, "No Place for Hate," which supports schools having a zero-tolerance policy for bullying. Schools can contact the Anti-Defamation League and can request the program's materials be sent to their school including lessons and posters. The overall objective of the program is to promote inclusivity and acceptance and to end bullying. Research has shown repeatedly that perpetrators of school violence are typically withdrawn and are usually victims of perpetual bullying. If bullied repeatedly, many students will feel the need to retaliate or use violence rather than expressing themselves verbally in order to regain power and control (Zuckerman, 2016). Thus, school counselors and key stakeholders must collaborate and educate parents, faculty, and students about the dire risks associated with bullying and the consequences. Counselors and stakeholders can teach students about the importance of being upstanders rather than bystanders, in that upstanders stand up for students being bullied rather than standby, observe, or ignore. Integrating antibullying programs such as Steps to Respect, No Place For Hate, or the Olweus Bullying Program can have a tremendously positive impact on mitigating bullying and assist stakeholders in formulating an inclusive, safe, connected, and accepting school climate, which is critical for student academic success and mental health.

Creating a Safe School Climate

Creating a safe and secure school climate is integral to SEL, as without having a cohesive climate, students will struggle academically, psychologically, socially, and emotionally. SEL emphasizes the importance of communication, conflict resolution, zest, optimism, and motivation; all of which are directly impacted by the degree of safety and security a school climate possesses. Stakeholders must work diligently to create a climate that is strength-based, student-centered, engaging, rigorous, and one in which students feel heard and validated, as this helps to motivate them to work toward their fullest potential. It is important for stakeholders to work to create a climate that is conducive to the needs of students (Cowan, Vaillancourt, Rossen & Pollitt, 2013), as this helps to increase engagement and connectivity. School counselors can do several things in order to enhance the overall school climate, and they are discussed in the following sections.

Conducting Needs Assessments

School counselors are trained to be data-driven practitioners. One of the most important questions school counselors ask is, 'How are students different as a result of our services?' In order to best meet students' needs, needs assessments can be conducted at the beginning of the school year in order to identify the most pressing needs, as well as to assess the impact of those needs on student outcomes. Needs Assessments can be conducted via paper and pencil or electronically via Qualtrics or another survey software. Needs Assessments can be administered to students, faculty, or parents to obtain data from key stakeholders in order to determine the major issues in the school that need to be addressed. Once needs are identified, interventions can then be developed and evaluated (program evaluations) in order to figure out the impact of the intervention on student learning outcomes. In addition to completing needs assessments, counselors can also create safety surveys for students to respond to in order to obtain and implement student and stakeholder feedback about how safe students feel at school (Bray, 2016).

Identifying At-Risk Students and Conducting Threat Assessments

Identifying at-risk students and conducting threat assessments is directly correlated to SEL in that SEL emphasizes the importance of school safety, mental health, emotion regulation, resolving conflicts peacefully, communication, and coping skills. Students who are at risk of carrying out acts of violence may lack these vital SEL skills and therefore engage in volatile behavior rather than verbal expression when dealing with internalized anger or sadness. In order to promote a safe and secure school climate, counselors can create advisory councils that include stakeholders in order to assess issues taking place at the school and community (Bray, 2016). As school counselors are not able to diagnose mental health disorders and refer out if a student is struggling with a diagnosed or undiagnosed mental health issue, the first step that needs to be taken in order to provide proper assistance is identifying students who may be struggling. Due to their high caseloads, counselors must work collaboratively with other stakeholders in order to determine students who may be struggling academically, lack social support, have a temper, have disciplinary issues, lack engagement, struggle with attendance, and lack coping skills, as these students have a higher propensity for carrying out acts of violence.

Conducting threat assessments is a vital component of protecting stakeholders, as threat assessments reflect the degree of risk a student may pose. Threat assessments are related to SEL, as they are indicative of the types of intrapersonal and interpersonal skills a student possesses. Threat assessments must be completed collaboratively, as all stakeholders who know the student need to be involved to share their perspectives. Asking questions about a student's access to weapons, frequency of disciplinary issues, struggles with mental health, support system, motives and goals, communication suggesting violence, and concern of others' regarding student's potential to engage in violence all need to be addressed in order to figure out the degree to which a student may pose a risk to self and others. Once a threat assessment is conducted and it is determined that a student poses a risk, parents need to be notified, resources need to be provided regarding mental health and wellness, referrals should be made for outside counseling if a student is struggling with deeper rooted issues, and authorities notified if a student has made direct threats about hurting self or others.

Fostering Resilience

Enhancing resilience and emphasizing that conflict is an inevitable part of life is critical so that students do not feel alone in their trials and tribulations. Resilience is one of the most vital SEL skills, as it reflects motivation, overcoming adversity, perseverance, optimism, and hope. Resilience addresses the importance for students to adapt, bounce back, and persevere through times of stress and difficulty. Counselors and key stakeholders work to encourage students to overcome challenges and to not allow challenges to dictate who they become. Increasing resilience is a pivotal piece of reducing school violence in that students who are resilient and have better coping skills, are more effective at resolving conflicts, are better able to regulate their emotions, as well as possess gratitude and hope for their future (Riopel, 2019). Stakeholders can help students augment their resilience by having an open-door policy, communicating, having school-wide and classroom conversations, emphasizing the importance of teachable moments; regardless of the outcome, we walk away stronger and wiser, to learn from failure and celebrate mistakes, as this helps to enhance learning, facilitate classroom, small group, and individual sessions on SE topics, as well as to teach students about motivation, mindset, optimism, and empowerment (Price-Mitchell, 2015). Students who are resilient have better coping skills and are less likely to experience feelings of intense stress and anxiety. Those who possess resilience, are more likely to assert themselves, lead, provide support, and help others who may be struggling academically or emotionally (Cassidy, 2015). Students who are resilient are more likely to engage in verbal communication to process struggles rather than lash out physically.

Increasing Parental Involvement and Monitoring Social Media

Research has substantiated consistently that parental involvement is instrumental for student success. Parental involvement is a fundamental aspect of SEL, as parents can work with their children at home to further enhance their SEL skills and parental involvement helps to increase connectivity, communication, engagement, resilience, empathy, and problem-solving. There is a strong and positive correlation between parental involvement and student achievement (Garcia & Thorton, 2014). Parental involvement is important for student learning and growth (Centers for Disease Control and Prevention, 2018). Parental involvement allows for improved student behavior, increased achievement, and well-developed social skills, as well as a reduction in at-risk behaviors (Centers for Disease Control and Prevention, 2018). Parents can work with their children on setting SMART goals (goals that are specific, measurable, achievable, realistic, and timely), enhance expectations, work collaboratively with their child's teacher to monitor grades and progress, as well as reach out to the school counselor or other stakeholders if they feel their child needs additional support. Parents who are engaged have children who achieve more, as well as experience enhanced motivation and communication skills. These skills help students to feel more connected, safer, and more focused, which in turn helps to reduce violence (Centers for Disease Control and Prevention, 2018). Counselors can include parents in the planning, share updates on their child's progress, and process any concerns they may have regarding academic, social emotional, or behavioral issues. Parents can also volunteer to be a part of formulating the school improvement or violence prevention plan, further enhancing collaboration (Bray, 2016). Parents can reinforce SEL skills at home by encouraging their children to be accountable, independent, and giving them leadership roles in order to enhance their communication and collaboration skills.

Moreover, parents play an instrumental role in monitoring their child's social media accounts (Bray, 2016). As previously stated, bullying and cyberbullying are leading causes of violence in schools, therefore closely monitoring students' social media accounts is pivotal in order to gauge the types of messages students are sending and receiving. Many times, at-risk students may post messages that are cryptic or alarming on social media rather than communicating in person. These messages may imply that they are threatening to hurt themselves or others. The messages MUST BE TAKEN SERIOUSLY AND REPORTED IMMEDIATELY. It is essential that parents are cognizant of what their children are posting or receiving so if the material is alarming, the parents can share their concerns with stakeholders in the school and community. Parents who are involved, proactive, vigilant, supportive, and influential can play an important role in reducing school violence (Centers for Disease Control and Prevention, 2018).

Celebrating Diversity

Celebrating diversity is a pivotal factor related to SEL, as this emphasizes cultural responsiveness, cultural sensitivity, acceptance, inclusion, collaboration, communication, and awareness. As many school perpetrators feel a sense of isolation, lack of support, anger, desire for retaliation, and exclusion, celebrating diversity can play a large role in mitigating school violence, as this helps to foster parental involvement, validation, understanding, acknowledgment, inclusivity, and acceptance. There are several strategies that schools can use to acknowledge diversity:

- Have parents come and speak to classes about the culture of origin in order to educate and enlighten students about various cultures.
- Hang flags in the school that represent all different cultures.
- Integrate culture and learning about cultures into core classes in order to enhance engagement and connectivity.
- Have students bring in a dish or artifact from their culture of origin to discuss with their class.
- Use differentiated learning instruction in order to meet the learning needs of all students.
- Work to challenge negative attitudes and bias, as this can lead to separation and judgments rather than cohesion and acceptance.
- Have open conversations about inequity in order to create a safe space for students to talk about how discrimination has impacted them, as this helps to foster change.
- **ISMs Activity:** Addressing various ISMs including RACISM, ANTI-SEMITISM, AGEISM, ABLEISM, CLASSISM, and SEXISM. Have students discuss a time when they or a person they know experienced one of these ISMs, how it has impacted them, and what they did to overcome this, as that helps to build inner strength, self-efficacy, and resilience.
- **Cross the Line Activity:** Educators can read off statements and if students have experienced the statement being read, they can cross the line. This activity allows for normalization, as well as recognition that although we are all different, we are more alike and have had similar experiences. This allows for trust and bonding to be built.
- **Culture Tree:** Using an image of a tree, students can identify their values/and beliefs on the roots of the tree, their cultural characteristics on the trunk of the tree, and their cultural groups (race, religion, ethnicity) on the leaves of the tree and then process in a large group in order to share similarities and differences.
- **Four Questions Activity:** Students can complete this activity in a large group and address describing themselves in regard to their heritage in four words, one time they have been aware of being one of those four words, one thing that is difficult or embarrassing about being one of those four words, and one thing that they are proud of in regard to their four chosen words used to describe themselves.
- **Stereotypes and Pride Activity:** Students will record five stereotypes that exist regarding their culture of origin, how the stereotypes have impacted them personally, as well as steps they have taken to overcome these stereotypes, which is very empowering and promotes a sense of control and validation.
- **Diversity Scavenger Hunt:** In which students can work in small groups and go outside to find materials that reflect diversity such as flowers, rocks, leaves. Students can then process in a large group the

importance of having diversity in the classroom, as well as the significance of celebrating differences and appreciating similarities between people.

• **See Me Activity:** Students can draw six eyes and inside of the eyes they can record what they believe other people think of them when they first see them based on their outside appearance and upon completion, students can process any discrepancies that exist between how they perceive other people to see them and how they actually see themselves.

Promoting cultural diversity is imperative in reducing school violence, as this helps to raise awareness, mitigate bias, promote understanding, enhance importance, self-control, sharing, educating, fosters open discussions, and helps stakeholders to address their struggles, triumphs, similarities, and differences.

Peer Pal System

Having a peer pal system is fundamentally important in regard to mitigating school violence. Utilizing peer pals underlies the importance of SEL in that this promotes collaboration, communication, peer support, togetherness, reduces isolation, promotes conflict resolution, enhances accountability, and increases social skill-building. Peers can be matched via grade level or age. Each student can be paired with a "peer pal" and throughout the day the students can interact when completing group work, if one student needs assistance, peer pals can eat together, or spend time together during Physical Education class. Assigning students peer pals can help students feel more accepted, help them to feel more supported, as well as provide an immediate support system if a student is struggling academically, behaviorally, or emotionally. If a peer is struggling, their pal can then share their concerns with their teacher or school counselor in order to offer additional support to the student. Additionally, peer pals can help to motivate one another and help one another be accountable and responsible for their own choices and behavior. Due to the fact that counselors have such a high caseload and teachers meet with numerous students throughout the day and are not able to interact with each student on an in-depth basis, having an assigned peer pal will help to identify students who may be presenting with at-risk behavior, as peer pals will work closely with one another and if one is struggling this will then be easier to identify and provide necessary resources to better support the student. Peer pals can be versatile and used in the K-12 setting in order to help foster a safer, more engaged, motivated, and inclusive school climate.

Peer Mediation

According to the Resolution Center (2019), peer mediation is a process that enables problem-solving by youth with youth. It is a process in which two or more students who are in an argument meet in a neutral and private setting and work out problems with a trained mediator. The purpose of peer mediation is for both students to demonstrate respect, listen actively to one another, share their stories, and work collaboratively to find resolve. Once resolution is reached, a contract can be signed indicating that the outcome will be abided by. Peer mediation reflects SEL in that it focuses on peaceful problem-solving, promotes accountability, empathy, compassion, communication, active listening, and collaboration between peers. Some advantages of peer mediation are that it has been shown to reduce the amount of time staff spend on disciplining, instead of using punitive punishment, students work together to find a resolution that both students agree to, and this process also helps to give students control and empowers them to resolve conflicts by themselves. Peer mediation helps to reinforce SEL skills and allows students to practice skills obtained to resolve conflicts in a proactive manner. The peer mediation process involves planning prior to the mediation, the mediator's introduction, both students sharing their perspectives, and then negotiation to resolve a problem. Students who are trained mediators are encouraged to demonstrate trustworthiness, approachability, dedication, perceptiveness, and neutrality (Piedmont Dispute Resolution Center, 2021). Integrating peer mediation can help to mitigate school violence in that students have the opportunity to talk to one another, feel validated and heard, take on leadership roles, and work with one another to resolve conflict in a peaceful and proactive way. Having a peer mediation program helps to reduce feelings regarding the need for retaliation (a leading cause of school violence), as problems are resolved and students feel empowered.

Visibility and Break Down Codes of Silence

Visibility is critical and underlies the importance of SEL, as visibility allows for trust, relationship building, and promoting healthy relationships between peers and faculty. Counselors must have visibility, as they work tirelessly as leaders, change agents, and advocates who have a presence throughout the school. This presence helps students to feel more comfortable talking to counselors about any concerns they may have (Bray, 2016). Having a familiar face of someone who is genuine and authentic, helps to foster connectivity amongst key stakeholders. In regard to reducing school violence, visibility is key, as students need to have stakeholders to talk to who are trained, possess a mental health background, and can provide support to students who are struggling (Bray, 2016). Counselors work collaboratively with other stakeholders to identify those who may be at risk. Research has substantiated that students may carry out acts of violence in order to be acknowledged and recognized (Bray, 2016). Counselors work intentionally to create a safe climate in which students feel engaged and included and through formulating connections via visibility. This helps students to feel heard, validated, and experience belonging, which in turn helps schools to be safer. In addition to being visible in order to amplify relationships and communication with students, breaking down codes of silence and in order to enhance communication is key. Many times students are aware of information or potential threats that they hear in the cafeteria, on the bus, after school, outside of school, or on social media that stakeholders may not be aware of. Therefore, breaking down codes of silence and encouraging students to come forward with information WITHOUT fear of retaliation is key in reducing school violence. The several strategies counselors can use to break down codes of silence are as follows:

Google Forms: Using Google Forms is an effective way for students, parents, and faculty to communicate directly with the counselor and make an appointment to speak with the counselor in a discreet and safe way. Counselors can create Google Forms and indicate

- A topic that needs to be discussed.
- The time that is conducive to meeting.
- The day that is convenient.
- Leave space for students/parents/faculty to elaborate on concerns.

Google Forms once completed go directly to the school counselor's inbox so they are made aware of a concern immediately. Google Forms can be used for everyday appointments, as well as for more dire concerns.

Worry Box: Worry Boxes are a very impactful way for students to share their concerns. A cardboard box with a slit in it can be left in the school counselor's office. Worries that are recorded can be done so either using identity disclosure or be completed anonymously just to let a counselor know that something alarming is taking place and that this needs to be addressed. Many times if students have the information they may not say anything out of fear of revenge. Thus, having the option of writing an anonymous worry can take that fear out of sharing information.

Conducting Assemblies on Mitigating Violence: School counselors are encouraged to facilitate schoolwide assemblies for all critical stakeholders including parents, administrators, faculty, and students. At the assemblies, counselors can discuss:

- The leading causes of violence (bullying, grief and loss, depression, retaliation).
- Characteristics of perpetrators.

- The importance of being an upstander rather than a bystander in regard to bullying.
- Communicating and sharing information regarding threats if made aware.
- Monitoring social media and **reporting on any** cryptic posts and threats.
- Importance of SEL in enhancing academic performance, and social/emotional/mental health and wellness.

References

Beland, L., & Kim, D. (2016). The effect of high school shootings on schools and student performance. *Educational Evaluation and Policy Analysis, 38*, 113–126.

Bray, C. (2016). *The counselor's role in ensuring school safety.* Retrieved from http://ct.counseling.org/2016/08/counselors-role-ensuring-school-safety/

Buchesky, S. (2018). *The answer to school violence is social emotional learning.* Retrieved from https://www.realcleareducation.com/articles/2018/06/12/the_answer_to_school_violence_is_social-emotional_learning_110283.html

Cassidy, S. (2015). *Resilience building in students: The role of academic self-efficacy.* Retrieved from https://www.frontiersin.org/articles/10.3389/fpsyg.2015.01781/full

Centers for Disease Control and Prevention (2018). *Parent engagement in schools.* Retrieved from https://www.cdc.gov/healthyyouth/protective/parent_engagement.htm

Center for Disease Control and Prevention (2019). *Preventing school violence.* Retrieved from https://www.cdc.gov/violenceprevention/youthviolence/schoolviolence/fastfact.html?CDC_AA_refVal=https%3A%2F%2Fwww.cdc.gov%2Fviolenceprevention%2Fyouthviolence%2Fschoolviolence%2Findex.html

Cowan, K. C., Vaillancourt, K., Rossen, E., & Pollitt, K. (2013). A framework for safe and successful schools. Retrieved from http://www.p12.nysed.gov/sss/documents/FrameworkforSafeandSuccessfulSchoolEnvironments_FINAL.pdf

Erickson, A. (2018). This is how common school shootings are in America. Retrieved from https://www.chicagotribune.com/opinion/commentary/ct-america-school-shootings-20180215-story.html

Everytown (2021). The impact of gun violence on children and teens. Retrieved from https://everytownresearch.org/report/the-impact-of-gun-violence-on-children-and-teens/

Everytown (2020). *Guns in schools.* Retrieved from https://www.everytown.org/issues/guns-in-schools/

Garcia, L. E., & Thorton, O. (2014). *The enduring importance of parental involvement.* Retrieved from https://www.region10.org/r10website/assets/File/The%20Enduring%20Importance%20of%20ParentalInvolvemen1.pdf

Kamentz, A. (2018). *Is there any way for schools to prevent shootings?* Retrieved from https://www.npr.org/sections/ed/2018/02/15/586022815/is-there-any-way-orschools-to-prevent-shootings

Mayo Clinic (2018). Oppositional Defiant Disorder. Retrieved from https://www.mayoclinic.org/diseases-conditions/oppositional-defiant-disorder/diagnosis-treatment/drc-20375837

National School Safety Center (2019). *Checklist of characteristics of youth who have caused school-associated violent deaths.* Retrieved from http://www. schoolsafety.us/media-resources/checklist-of-characteristics-of-youth-who-have-caused-school-associated-violent-deaths

Piedmont Dispute Resolution Center (2021). Conflict resolution, peer mediation, and restorative justice training. Retrieved from https://piedmontdisputeresolution.org/services/youth-and-schools/

Price-Mitchell, M. (2015). *Resilience: The capacity to rebuild and grow from adversity.* Retrieved from https://www.psychologytoday.com/us/blog/the-momentyouth/201507/resilience-the-capacity-rebuild-and-grow-adversity

Riopel, L. (2019). *Resilience skills, factors, and strategies of the resilient person.* Retrieved from https://positivepsychology.com/resilience-skills/

Simckes, M. (2017). *A dangerous mix: Bullied youth report access to loaded guns more than other youth.* Retrieved from https://theconversation.com/a-dangerous-mixbullied-youth-report-access-to-loaded-guns-more-than-other-youth-79619

Statista Research Department (2022). As of December 2021, there have been 249 school shootings in the United States Number of K-12 school shootings in the United States from 1970 to December 2021 by active shooter status. Retrieved from https://www.statista.com/statistics/971473/number-k-12-school-shootings-us/

Studer, J. R., & Salter, S. E. (2010). *Role of the school counselor in crisis planning and intervention.* Retrieved from https://www.counseling.org/resources/library/vistas/2010-V-Online/Article_92.pdf

The Resolution Center (2019). *Mediation training for today & for the future.* Retrieved from http://www.theresolutioncenter.com/training/

Teasley, M. L. (2018). School shootings and the need for more school based mental health services. *Children & Schools*, 40, 131–134.

Young, A. (2019). *From doer to leader.* Retrieved from https://www.ascaschoolcounselor-digital.org/ascaschoolcounselor/november_december_2019/MobilePagedArticle.action?articleId=1536790#articleId1536790

Zuckerman, D. (2016). *Bullying harms victims and perpetrators of all ages.* Retrieved from https://www.chausa.org/publications/health-progress/article/july-august-2016/bullying-harms-victims-and-perpetrators-of-all-ages

14 Social Emotional Learning
School-Wide Programs

Positive Behavior Intervention and Support

Positive Behavior Intervention and Support is not a social emotional learning (SEL) program per se, but it does directly help to enhance learning and behavioral outcomes. Positive behavior intervention and support (PBIS) is an evidence-based three-tiered framework used to improve student outcomes. In Tier I, practices are universal and proactive support is implemented in order to improve behaviors and academics school-wide. In Tier 2, practices are more intentional and students who are at risk for developing more serious behavioral issues receive support before the behaviors start; being proactive. The skills learned help students to be successful in school. In Tier 3, students receive more intensive and individualized support in order to enhance their behavioral and academic outcomes (Center on PBIS, 2021). Additionally, within PBIS mental health and wellness are addressed across all settings and are found in curricula. Schools use data to ensure that SEL and behavioral competencies are at the focus of each of the three PBIS Tiers. Using PBIS allows for a continuum of evidence-based interventions, use of data at every tier in order to monitor student growth, screening, and monitoring (Center on PBIS, 2021). In order to address mental health in Tier 1, school and community clinicians address SEL and behavioral needs of all students. In Tier 2, stakeholders work to connect students to various targeted interventions addressing social skills, problem-solving skills, and coping skills; especially for students who may be struggling with anxiety or depression. In Tier 3, school-based and community clinicians develop more individualized interventions in order to provide support to struggling students. Thus, PBIS is critical for student success and reducing school violence, as it integrates SEL for all students and works to identify students who are struggling early on in order to provide immediate support.

No Place For Hate

The Anti-Defamation League (2021) has created the No Place for Hate program in order to combat bullying and bias and stop the escalation of

DOI: 10.4324/9781003262183-14

hate. It is a self-directed program that helps to promote an equitable, respectful, and inclusive school climate. The program is customizable to meet the needs of individual students and it follows a four-phase approach including forming a committee to promote change, signing a pledge to commit to having a zero-tolerance policy for bullying, assessing the school's climate, and motivating students and staff to become allies through activity implementation. The program is free of cost and posters, lesson plans, and books are used to reinforce equity, peace, empathy, and respect for all. One aspect of No Place for Hate that is so important is that this program can be implemented at all levels P-12 and is very versatile. This program is **STRONGLY** recommended in regard to reducing bullying and school violence.

Olweus Antibullying/Violence Prevention Program

The Olweus Bullying Prevention Program is one of the most widely used and researched antibullying programs. It is a whole-school program that has been shown to prevent or reduce bullying. All students and adults participate and can be used in elementary, middle, and high school. The program's goals are to improve peer relationships, reduce bullying, prevent the development of future bullying, and have enhanced outcomes for students. The Olweus Bullying Program includes school-, classroom-, individual-, and community-level components (Hazelden Foundation, 2016). The program focuses on mitigating bullying and violence prevention in the schools via training, involvement, and integrating SEL components into instruction.

Steps to Respect

Steps to Respect is an antibullying program for grades 3–6. The program addresses character education and SEL in order to end bullying. The program is designed to increase staff awareness and responsiveness, to help foster socially responsible ideas and beliefs, teach SEL in order to combat bullying, and help build healthy relationships. The program also addresses conflict resolution in order to overcome bullying. The program reiterates the importance of being an upstander rather than a bystander, helps to enhance social competence, and enhances respectful behavior. Research has shown that improved social skills lead to reduced bullying and safer school climates (youth.gov, 2021).

The 4 R's Program

This program has been developed for students P-5 and there is an emphasis on reading, writing, respect, and finding resolve. SEL is incorporated via literature. There are 35 lessons and 7 units. The material helps students to understand their own culture, as well as educates students about a variety of cultures in order to promote enlightenment, diversity, and enhance social skill-building. Research has shown that schools who have utilized this program have shown increases in social competence, academic scores, lower regression and bias, and an improved classroom climate in regard to engagement and connectivity (Brown, Jones, LaRusso, & Aber, 2010).

Caring School Community (CSC)

This program has been developed for students K-6th grade and focuses on enhancing the classroom and school community, as well as teaching SEL skills. CSC is school-wide and there are 35 lessons that encourage using school buddies, doing home activities in order to foster family involvement, problem-solving, building social skills, and decision-making. There are class meetings that enable students to complete various activities related to themes being addressed. The buddy program has shown to enhance social skill-building. The program focuses on interpersonal skill-building, cognitive regulation, emotional processes, character; all integral components for mitigating bullying and school violence, as well as amplifying student success (Center for the Collaborative Classroom, 2019)

Character First

A P-12 program that focuses on character education and positive social values that are important for good citizenship, responsibility, building social skills, communication, and collaboration. The program is made up of 20-character traits and separate predeveloped lessons for each grade level. Usually, one character trait is focused on per month including courage, determination, kindness, compassion, empathy, diligence, flexibility, honesty, patience, respect, and self-control. The program focuses on fostering a growth mindset, character building, and enhancing interpersonal skills. Character education is monumentally important for reducing bullying and school violence, as these programs teach and instill knowledge and values in students at a young age addressing the importance of togetherness, friendship, acceptance, and empathy. Other impactful character education programs include **Character Counts** and **Learning for Life**; both manualized and comprehensive in providing solid character education for youth. Speaking from personal experience, when I worked as a school counselor years ago, I implemented the Learning for Life program at the elementary school I worked at and the program helped to significantly reduce bullying incidents, as well as behavioral referrals.

Lions Quest

Lions Quest is a P-12 program that emphasizes SEL, character education, bullying prevention, and anti-substance usage. As the students get older, the concepts require more critical thinking. Each lesson is approximately 30minutes in length. The program addresses cognitive regulation, emotional processes, interpersonal skills, character, and mindset. Research has shown that participants have experienced enhanced self-efficacy, self-assertion, confidence, reduction in substance usage, and less bullying (Drolet, Arcand, Ducharme, & Leblanc, 2013).

Botvin Life Skills Training

Evidence-based programs are used in 39 countries worldwide in order to reduce bullying, substance usage, tobacco, and school violence. The program helped to reduce substance usage amongst students by 75%, alcohol use by 60% violence by 50%, and tobacco by 87% (Botvin Lifeskills Training, 2021). Botvin's Life Skills Training is offered in elementary, middle, and high school. Botvin's Life Skills Training integrates SEL in order to help students develop enhanced self-worth, decreased anxiety, increased self-confidence, and more impactful problem-solving and decision-making skills. The program integrates technology and interactive components in order to make it more engaging for students. The Botvin Lifeskills Training program is empirically based and effective in creating safer, healthier, and more responsive school climates.

Responsive Services: Classroom/Small Group/Individual Counseling

The American School Counselor Association (ASCA) created national student: Mindsets and Behaviors for student success in order to create standards and competencies universally to ensure that all students will receive assistance in enhancing SEL skills to promote life readiness (ASCA, 2021). School counselors receive intensive training to help students develop growth mindsets, in which skills and learning are enhanced via practice and if given the resources to do so, as well as help students to enhance their behaviors in order to create a school climate that is college and career ready and secure (ASCA, 2021). School counselors incorporate SEL into their direct services in order to help students augment their problem-solving, emotion regulation, communication, accountability, leadership, assertiveness, and interpersonal skills. SEL embodies acquiring and applying knowledge and attitudes necessary to understand and regulate emotions, set and accomplish positive goals, show empathy, establish healthy relationships, and make sound choices (CASEL, 2021) and these core abilities are critical for students to possess in order to reduce volatility in schools.

Core SEL skills that have been shown to enhance student success include motivation, self-efficacy, autonomy, peer relationships, conflict resolution, and emotion regulation. SEL helps students to be more aware, better able to manage behaviors, more socially aware, more able to create healthy relationships, and more capable of making healthy choices. In order to help students reach their fullest potential, counselors can integrate intrapersonal and interpersonal skills including emotion regulation, anger management, time and stress management, conflict resolution, leadership, assertiveness, resilience, empathy, and collaboration into their comprehensive counseling curricula in order to help students experience greater self-control, empowerment, feelings of validation, as well as unconditional acceptance. The underlying motivation for integrating SEL into curricula is to help students process and express themselves verbally and constructively rather than through destructive or violent means.

There are several SEL topics that counselors can conduct classroom/ small group/or individual counseling sessions on in order to create a more secure climate that is conducive to learning and success including:

Anger Management: Many perpetrators who carry out acts of violence struggle with anger management issues, depression, lack of coping skills, resentment, and desire for revenge (Bray, 2016). Counselors can facilitate small groups addressing anger management and can work with students to help them process their anger in constructive and effective ways. Counselors can help students learn counting, deep breathing techniques, meditation, cognitive restructuring in which students learn to positive reframe and reword unhealthy thoughts, identify triggers of anger, and ways to better cope with causes of anger. Counselors can do creative activities to help students better manage their anger. Counselors can also integrate anger management programs such as the Anger Coping program that enables students to mitigate their anger so that it does not consume them (Furlong, Felix, Sharkey, & Larson, 2005). Additionally, when counselors are working with students who are struggling with anger management issues they can do the following:

- **Anger Bag:** Using a brown paper bag, students can decorate the paper bag with words, images, colors, and shapes that reflect anger.
  - On strips of paper, students can record triggers of anger.
  - Students can then process their triggers of anger out loud and upon completion crumple them up and throw them into their anger bag as a way to purge and release their anger.

- **Anger Flower:** On a flower cutout, in the middle of the flower students can write, "I Can Relax By ..." and on the petals of the flower students can record ways they can de-escalate including deep breathing, going for a walk, listening to music, squeezing hands).
- **Anger Scale:** Students can rate on a scale from 1 to 5 (1 being low and 5 being high) how angry they are feeling. Students can then draw a picture of how they look when they are feeling angry, as well as describe how they are feeling. Students can then be asked, "What

would need to happen in order for you to reduce your anger from a 4 to a 3?" Students can then process what they can do autonomously to help themselves feel less anger.

• Processing anger is essential, as when anger is internalized this can lead to feelings of sadness and depression.

Conflict Resolution: It is imperative for counselors to facilitate groups related to conflict resolution either in the classroom, small group setting or individually, as students need to be aware of how to problem-solve peacefully in order to have a win–win outcome for both people involved (Cromwell, 2012). The Conflict Resolution Education Report (Cromwell, 2012) addresses creating a climate in which students feel safe and can focus on their achievements. Mediation, negotiation, and consensus of decision-making are three major components that encompass conflict resolution (Cromwell, 2012). Conflict resolution is vital for peaceful schools, as students must possess the skills necessary to problem-solve and to process issues verbally rather than to use violence or excessive force, as that does not solve anything it only causes more turmoil. The Peace Education Foundation is a conflict resolution program that gives information on conflict resolution and problem-solving for K-12 students. The Peaceable Classroom Approach is another conflict resolution program that helps to teach cooperative learning methods to problem-solving. The Resolving Conflict Creatively Program integrates parent involvement and, peer mediation, and conflict resolution into classroom teaching (Cromwell, 2012). Conflict resolution is fundamentally important today as there are constant conflicts. Since we live in a society in which technology is pervasive, students need to learn foundational communication, listening skills, and enhance their open-mindedness in order to see and understand a variety of viewpoints (Confident Counselors, 2019). Teaching students to actively listen, to use eye contact and appropriate nonverbal skills, and to work together when problem-solving is vital so that students learn to solve problems both in school, as well as in the workforce. Conflict resolution skills help angry students to redirect their anger and to express themselves in a confident way rather than deflecting or blaming others for their feelings (Confident Counselors, 2019). In regard to conflict resolution, both people involved must understand what the argument is about, establish a common goal, address ways to meet the goal, determine barriers to achieving the goal, and agree on the best way to resolve the conflict. As conflict is inevitable and unavoidable, understanding conflict resolution styles including (University of Notre Dame, 2020)

• Avoiding Conflict: Not partaking in conflict and the pretending issue does not exist.
• Giving In: One person accommodates or gives in to the other person and accepts his/her point of view without addressing one's own.

- Standing Your Ground: One person is essentially competing with the other in order to "win" the battle. This is a competitive approach and can have detrimental outcomes, as no one wins.
- Compromising: Positive step towards resolution in which both people involved in the conflict seek common ground and begin to negotiate toward resolution.
- Collaborating: Significant part of conflict resolution, as both people are working together effectively to solve a problem. Collaborating involves listening, discussing, and making sure people understand one another.

In regard to helping students enhance their conflict resolution skills:

- Peer mediation is very powerful, as this allows peers to work with their peers to help facilitate problem-solving.
- Using role-plays can be effective in allowing students to work together to practice resolving conflict.
- Teaching students to walk away if they are too upset and to come back together once they have both calmed down.
- Addressing aggressive (volatile) versus assertive (confident/straight-forward) behavior.
- Processing the importance of forgiveness.
- Addressing accountability in that each person involved needs to be responsible for their actions and is encouraged to think about what they can do differently in the future if they face a similar conflict.

Conflict resolution skills are paramount for students to possess in regard to creating a safe school climate, as they help to build relationships, enhance communication, are goal-driven, and enable students to process, communicate, and work to resolve problems peacefully so that they do not intensify or become destructive.

Accountability

Accountability is a monumentally important skill to teach in schools; specifically in regard to mitigating bullying and school violence. Accountability is a core SEL skill, as it focuses on the importance of personal responsibility, self-reflection, ownership rather than deflection. In order to reduce school violence, students MUST be accountable for their actions and recognize that actions have consequences. The importance here is helping students to identify teachable moments. We all make mistakes. The significance is to learn from mistakes so we can do better moving forward. There is always room for growth. Like all SEL skills, accountability can be taught and enhanced. Counselors can conduct classroom, small group, or individual counseling sessions addressing accountability. When students are accountable, they are able to see their role in a situation and can assess what was effective, what was ineffective, and determine what can be done differently moving forward. Additionally, there are several skills counselors can teach students in order to be more accountable including:

> **I Messages:** "I Messages" are important for accountability and assertiveness, as they allow students to express themselves in a confident manner and take ownership of their feelings. I feel _____ when you _____ because _____. Please stop. By using an "I Message," students can learn to express themselves and communicate their feelings in a straight forward manner. "I Messages" allow students to take responsibility for their feelings rather than blame or shame others (Martin, 2004). Having students practice using "I Messages" is important so that they can become familiar with the format and practice taking ownership of their feelings (Martin, 2004).
> **Reflective Practice:** Reflective practice allows for people to assess their strengths, as well as their areas for growth. Reflective practice is a key component of accountability, as this allows students to reflect upon and consider their role in a conflict or situation, how they acted, and what they can potentially to differently in the future in order to experience a more positive outcome.
> **Apologizing:** It is important to teach students how to apologize if they do something to intentionally or unintentionally hurt another. Apologizing shows that a student is taking accountability and that they recognize that their action was wrong. It allows for under-standing, builds empathy, and fosters personal responsibility.
> **Lead by Example:** Teach students to lead by example and act as role models; with integrity, strength, compassion, and discipline. By leading with example, other students will emulate that behavior and be inspired to also demonstrate accountability and leadership.

Being accountable also helps to enhance empathy. This allows students to have a deeper and more meaningful understanding of what another may be going through and that helps to belong, inclusion, and acceptance; all critical qualities for reducing school violence. Being accountable and responsible for actions is integral for growth and for creating a peaceful school climate.

Empathy

Empathy is one of the most imperative SEL skills, and without empathy re-lationships, morale, self-awareness, accountability, leadership, compassion, emotion regulation, conflict resolution, and decision-making all suffer. Empathy is instrumental to SEL, as it epitomizes relationship building, self, and other awareness, perspective taking, resolving problems, communicating, collaborating, optimism, and motivation. Counselors can facilitate classroom, small group, or individual counseling sessions addressing empathy, as it helps students to take on emotions of others as if they were their own and to put themselves in that person's shoes and imagine what that person may be going through. Empathy is a vitally important skill to possess in school and in life in order to truly connect with and build relationships with others. Empathy is important for students to be productive in school and at home (Harvard School of Education, 2018). Empathy helps to foster classroom engagement, academic achievement, behaviors, improves communication skills, helps to build positive relationships, as well as works to decrease aggressive behaviors (Harvard School of Education, 2018). Being empathic helps to mitigate school violence, as students can visualize the emotions of others and consider the impact of their actions on others, allowing them to be proactive rather than reactive. Increasing empathy may also help to enhance moral identity, self-reflection, perspective sharing, and togetherness (Borba, 2018). Through building empathy, students may become more compassionate, less impulsive, more intentional, thoughtful, and more self-aware. There are several ways counselors can help students build empathy:

> **Walk in My Shoes:** Counselors can cut out an image of a shoe. Inside the shoe students can write down a challenge they have faced. Upon completion, counselors can ask students how they would feel if they went through that experience and what they would do to overcome the challenge. This activity helps to build empathy, perspective taking, communication, self-disclosure, and understanding.
> **Role Plays:** Counselors can share vignettes of challenges or have students act out a relatable challenge. The other students who are observing and the students in the role play can then process emotions experienced, the impact of the situation on the student's self-concept, as well as what can be done to overcome the challenge in order to experience empowerment. Role playing is a wonderful technique to use, as it allows for modeling, as well as practicing skills learned.
> **Feelings Collage:** Students can collaboratively or individually create a feelings collage composed of words, quotes, or images that reflect their emotions. Upon completion, students can share their collage and process how they are feeling and triggers of those emotions. Students can then process collaboratively healthy ways to deal with emotions they may each be experiencing.
> **Modeling:** Modeling can help students to be more empathic. When parents and faculty demonstrate empathy, students can then model this behavior and become more empathic themselves. Parents and faculty can model empathy by identifying emotions, asking questions about feelings, demonstrating kindness and compassion, and pro-viding constructive feedback, as that demonstrates investment and caring in regard to personal and professional growth.

Decision-Making

Decision-making is an essential SEL skill in regard to mitigating gun violence, as students who may be struggling emotionally or mentally may be in a fight or flight state that is impeding upon their ability to make healthy, rational, and constructive decisions. Many times students who are going through a difficult time may struggle with making healthy choices or have difficulty recognizing the impact of their choices on others, as they are in a complete state of despair. Therefore, it is significant for counselors to teach decision-making skills so that students can learn impactful ways to make healthy choices. Counselors can facilitate classroom, small group, or individual counseling sessions addressing decision-making. Students are constantly making decisions about peers, pressures, goals they want to set, their post-secondary endeavors, their relationships, their academics, their families, and they must possess effective decision-making skills in order to be successful in school and in life. Counselors can work with students on the importance of weighing the pros and cons or the advantages and disadvantages of a situation in order to make them more informed choices. Facilitating groups on decision-making can help students to enhance their awareness and help them to make choices that best serve the students themselves and others around them (CASEL, 2021). Some strategies counselors can use to help students increase their decision-making skills include the following:

> **Decision Trees:** Students can draw a tree and on the branches of the tree students can record various options they have. On the outside of the tree, students can then record the possible outcomes of those options in order to assess the advantages and disadvantages to make the most informed choice.
>
> **Logical Consequences**: Logical consequences are an impactful counseling strategy to use when helping students work on their decision-making skills. Logical consequences follow this template: Tell me what will happen if you do this…. /Tell me what will happen if you do NOT do this… By verbally processing their options out loud in a collaborative manner, this can help students make the most advantageous decision.

Emotion Regulation

Emotion regulation reflects being in control, demonstrating self-discipline, and self-restraint. Emotion regulation is an important SEL in regard to reducing gun violence and bullying, as many times perpetrators of violence may be victims of relentless bullying, experience continuous disciplinary issues, may have had a recent loss, may lack coping skills, and as a result may act impulsively and lose control of their behavior, being reactive rather than proactive. It is monumentally important to teach students about emotion regulation and ways to regulate their emotions so when they become upset, frustrated, or angry, they are able to verbally and peacefully express their feelings rather than physically or aggressively. Counselors can address emotion regulation during the classroom, small group, or individual counseling so that students experience greater control over their emotions. Emotion regulation allows students to think before they act and to consider possible consequences of their behavior (Cuncic, 2019). School counselors can teach students better emotion regulation using the following techniques:

Mindfulness: Mindfulness involves being grounded, centered, and focused on the present here and now, rather than the past or future. Mindfulness can be done briefly at the beginning, middle, or end of a class or before transitioning to a new task. Students can close their eyes for 30 seconds or 1 minute, take deep breaths in, and notice how their body is feeling. Upon completion, they can open their eyes and experience being more focused and attentive. Mindfulness allows people to be intensely aware of what they are sensing in a specific moment without judgement. Practicing mindfulness can include breathing activities, guided imagery, and other ways to relax the mind and body (Mayo Clinic, 2021).

Cognitive Reframing: Reframing is a Cognitive Behavioral Therapy technique that allows people to challenge or reframe negative thoughts into more positive and healthy thoughts. There is a direct relationship between the impact of our thoughts have on our behaviors. Thus, if we think more positively our behaviors will reflect this. Cognitive reframing greatly enhances mental health, as people are able to see things from a different vantage point. Anytime people experience a distorted thought, they can engage in reframing to see this in a more positive light. For instance, if someone is struggling with a mental health issue, this can be reframed as having a reminder to take care of themselves every day (Morin, 2021). Rather than seeing a mental health issue as a stigma, by reframing this, we are able to **embrace, normalize, and destigmatize** mental health and use it as a tool to drive us forward to being the best that we can be and to take care of ourselves. A huge part of mitigating violence in schools is about making a paradigm shift and reframing in our minds about mental health and wellness. There need to be more counselors in order to serve an increased number of students who may be struggling and we need to understand like any other illness that mental health impacts everyone, is treatable, and educators must use their platform to address these issues, as the sooner we are able to intervene and support, the more successful the student, the school, and society at large will be. There is a monumental need to further normalize, destigmatize, educate, and raise awareness about mental health in order to truly make a lasting change.

Counting to Ten: Counting can be an impactful way to enhance emotion regulation. Through counting students are able to demonstrate better self-control and calmness, as they are able to de-escalate their emotions while counting. This allows students time to process how they are feeling and to be mindful of how they are feeling in the moment, allowing them to be proactive rather than reactive.

Emotion Freedom Technique: The Emotion Freedom Technique is used as a tool to help students enhance their self-regulation and decrease anxiety or stress. Students can use the Emotion Freedom Technique by tapping on various acupressure points on their body. This technique can be done discreetly at their desk allowing students to self-soothe and calm down independently.

Calm Down Corner: In a counselor's office or teacher's room, educators can have a specific area to allow students to regulate their emotions to experience calmness. Play-Doh, other tactile objects, and soothing music can be played for students to go to in order to help them calm down and better control their emotions autonomously without distracting other students. This can be very empowering for students, as they see that they have the ability to help themselves calm down when feeling upset.

Grief and Loss

Grief and loss is a driving force in bullying and school violence. Many perpetrators carrying out acts of violence have been found to have recently experienced some type of grief and loss whether it be loss of a relationship, loss of a pet, loss of a family member, parents' divorce, or some type of loss in their lives that they are struggling to cope with. Many students who carry out acts of violence lack proper coping skills to deal with loss and therefore may act out in a volatile way rather than a socially acceptable or healthy way. It is imperative for counselors to teach students healthy coping skills and strategies to use when dealing with grief and loss. It is known that there is not a universal way to deal with grief and grief has several stages including

- **Shock and Denial:** It is hard to believe the person we lost is gone and we need to adjust to a new reality, which can be very lonely and painful that we no longer have part of our support system. When experiencing denial, people do not want to focus on the loss and are trying to absorb what is happening (Verywell Mind, 2021).
- **Anger:** Many feel angry after experiencing the loss of someone they loved. Anger allows people to express an emotion with less fear of judgment or rejection. Anger can lead to feeling isolated and makes it

even more challenging to navigate loss alone. Anger, when internalized, leads to sadness and depression (Verywell Mind, 2021).

- **Bargaining**: Involves wanting to go back and change the outcome or prevent the loss. People may feel desperate when dealing with a loss and are willing to do anything to minimize the pain they are experiencing. Bargaining can include making promises in order to save the person we are losing or have lost. However, as humans, we recognize that are times we are helpless and experience feeling out of control as we realize there is nothing that we could do to stop the loss from occurring.
- **Depression:** Allows when people start to look at their new reality and the loss of their loved one is unavoidable. Sadness mounts and people may become more isolated and less social really struggling to cope with the loss (Verywell Mind, 2021).
- **Acceptance:** Sometimes people can be accepting of a loss and learn to coexist with the loss and sometimes people never accept the loss. When people reach the stage of acceptance they learn to not resist the reality of their loss (Verywell Mind, 2021).

In regard to grief and loss, there are several techniques counselors can use to help students more effectively cope including

Empty Chair Technique: Using the Empty Chair technique with students can be very helpful. Students can talk to an 'empty chair' and communicate with the person who they lost and share what they never had a chance to say. This is a powerful activity that can provide a sense of peace and closure.

Letter Writing: Writing is another impactful technique to use when grieving. Many times, students' emotions are so raw, that they have difficulty expressing themselves verbally. Therefore, writing a letter allows students to express themselves in written form and they are able to communicate and externalize their feelings of sadness and despair on paper. This can be very cathartic.

Coping Skills Jar: Students can decorate a plastic cup with words or images that reflect health and wellness in regard to coping. On individual popsicle sticks, students can record various coping skills that they can use when struggling. For instance, students can write down on different popsicle sticks exercising, reading, walking, talking, listening to music, art work, deep breathing. Students can choose a popsicle stick if struggling and can use the coping skill they chose in order to feel better.

Balloon Release: Students and counselors can work together and use balloons to celebrate and honor the lives of those students have lost. On balloons students can record what they loved most about the person. Students and counselors can then go outside and release the balloons into air in order to experience closure, liberation, and promise to carry on the person's legacy.

In order to reduce bullying and violence in schools, school counselors must teach and integrate SEL intrapersonal and interpersonal skills into their curricula in order to promote communication, collaboration, self-control, coping skills, hope and optimism, problem-solving, and accountability amongst students. SEL skills can be learned and amplified via practice. Gun violence has a deleterious impact on stakeholders' lives. There are a variety of strategies school counselors can use to mitigate gun violence including facilitating classroom, small group, and individual counseling sessions addressing SEL topics. Although they have high caseloads, counselors are strongly encouraged to collaborate with critical stakeholders including administrators, parents, and teachers in order to identify and provide support to at-risk students who demonstrate the proclivity to hurt themselves or others. Counselors must work diligently to create a safe climate that is rigorous, engaging, strength-based, accepting, and inclusive in order to promote unity and peace. Students who feel a sense of belonging, feel valued, safe, and connected to others are happier and more well-adjusted. Through developing a safe climate, students can feel more comfortable coming forward if they possess information about threats or disconcerting messages. Through facilitating classroom, small group, and individual counseling sessions addressing SEL topics including empathy, conflict resolution, anger management, motivation, optimism, emotion regulation, communication, diversity, collaboration, grief and loss, coping skills, and time and stress management, this helps students to feel more competent, confident, engaged, accepted, and more equipped to overcome life's challenges. School counselors have the unique ability to identify, assist, motivate, and empower students, and provide them with the tools and resources that they need to be their best selves. It is paramount that school counselors educate, provide vital responsive services, create a safe climate that is inspiring, and work tenaciously to provide resources so that all students have the opportunity to thrive, survive, succeed, and be victorious.

References

American School Counseling Association (2021). ASCA student standards: Mindsets and behaviors for student success. Retrieved from https://www.schoolcounselor.org/getmedia/7428a787-a452-4abb-afec-d78ec77870cd/Mindsets- Behaviors.pdf

Anti-Defamation League (2021). No place for hate. Retrieved from https://www.adl.org/who-we-are/our-organization/signature-programs/no-place-for-hate

Borba, M. (2018). *Nine competencies for teaching empathy*. Retrieved from http://www.ascd.org/publications/educational-leadership/oct18/vol76/num02/Nine-Competencies-for-Teaching-Empathy.aspx

Botvin Life Skills Training, (2021). LST overview. Retrieved from https://www. lifeskillstraining.com/lst-overview/

Bray, C. (2016). *The counselor's role in ensuring school safety.* Retrieved from http://ct.counseling.org/2016/08/counselors-role-ensuring-school-safety/

Brown, J. L., Jones, S. M., LaRusso, M. D., & Aber, J. L. (2010). Improving classroom quality: Teacher influences and experimental impacts of the 4Rs program. *Journal of Educational Psychology, 102*, 153–167.

Collaborative for Academic, Social, and Emotional Learning (CASEL) (2021). *What is SEL?* Retrieved from https://casel.org/fundamentals-of-sel/

Center for the Collaborative Classroom (2019). *Caring school community: Principles and structures to develop social skills.* Retrieved from https://www. collaborativeclassroom.org/programs/caring-school-community/

Center on Positive Behavior Intervention and Supports (2021). *Tiered framework.* Retrieved from https://www.pbis.org/pbis/tiered-framework

Confident Counselors (2019). *Teaching conflict resolution: Strategies for school counselors.* Retrieved from https://confidentcounselors.com/2019/04/04/teachingconflict-resolution/

Cromwell, S. (2012). *Conflict resolution education: Compare approaches.* Retrieved from https://www.educationworld.com/a_curr/curr171.shtml

Cuncic, A. (2019). How to develop and practice self-regulation. Retrieved from https://www.verywellmind.com/how-you-can-practice-self-regulation-4163536

Drolet, M., Arcand, I., Ducharme, D., & Leblanc, R. (2013). The sense of school belonging and implementation of a prevention program: Toward healthier interpersonal relationships among early adolescents. *Journal of Child Adolescent Social Work, 6*, 535–551.

Furlong, M. J., Felix, E. D., Sharkey, J. D., & Larson, J. (2005). Preventing school violence: A plan for safe and engaging schools. *Student Counseling*, 11–15.

Harvard School of Education (2018). *For educators: How to build empathy and strengthen your school community.* Retrieved from https://mcc.gse.harvard.edu/ resources-for-educators/how-build-empathy-strengthen-school-community

Hazelden Foundation (2016). *Violence prevention works: A foundation for healthier youth.* Retrieved from https://www.violencepreventionworks.org/public/ bullying.page

Martin, A. (2004). I messages & the assertiveness line. Retrieved from https://www. morningsidecenter.org/teachable-moment/lessons/i-messages-assertiveness-line

Mayo Clinic (2021). *Mindfulness exercises.* Retrieved from https://www.mayoclinic. org/healthy-lifestyle/consumer-health/in-depth/mindfulness-exercises/art-20046356

Morin, A. (2021). What is cognitive reframing? Retrieved from https://www. verywellmind.com/reframing-defined-2610419#:~:text=Cognitive%20reframing %20is%20a%20technique,from%20a%20slightly%20different%20perspective.

University of Notre Dame (2020). *The five styles of conflict resolution.* Retrieved from https://www.notredameonline.com/resources/negotiations/the-five-styles-of-conflict-resolution/

Verywell Mind (2021). *The five stages of grief.* Retrieved from https://www. verywellmind.com/five-stages-of-grief-4175361

Youth.gov (2021). *Steps to respect.* Retrieved from https://youth.gov/content/ steps-respect%C2%AE

15 Self-Awareness

Self-awareness involves feelings, interests, strengths, areas for growth, and exuding self-confidence and belief in oneself. A key component of self-awareness is being able to recognize and conceptualize emotions, as well as their causes and triggers (Mayer, Salovey, & Caruso, 2004).

Self-awareness includes having an understanding of one's own emotions and values, as well as assessing one's strengths, thoughts, feelings, and actions and how each is interconnected (Weissberg, 2016).

Self-awareness highlights one's intrinsic motivation and levels of self-pride when goals are attained. This competency relates to one's self-efficacy; the belief that one has that he or she can achieve his or her fullest potential (Bandura, Barbaranelli, Caprara, & Pastorelli, 2001). The following are lessons concentrating on the concept of Self-Awareness.

Secondary Activities

Lesson Plan 1: Anxiety

Directions: This activity can be facilitated in a classroom, small group, or individual counseling setting. First, the definition of anxiety will be addressed. Students will then process open-ended questions, complete the evidence-based practice activity, the creative activity, follow-up discussion questions in order to review material learned, as well as feedback questions to assess the impact of session on student learning outcomes.

Definition of Anxiety: A feeling of worry, nervousness, or unease about an upcoming event or something with an uncertain outcome.

Open-Ended Process Questions:

What words come to mind when you hear the word anxiety?
Fear, Worry, Concern
In what ways does anxiety impact us academically, socially, and emotionally?
Poor grades, isolation, fear, worry

DOI: 10.4324/9781003262183-15

Please share causes of anxiety in your life...
School/work/family/friends
Share healthy coping strategies we can use when feeling anxious...
Deep breathing, exercise, meditation

Evidence-Based Practice 1
GAD-7 in order to obtain a baseline measure of the level of students' anxiety https://adaa.org/sites/default/files/GAD-7_Anxiety-updated_0.pdf

Evidence-Based Practice 2
Emotion Freedom Tapping Technique
https://www.youtube.com/watch?v=Hfpl6WYBFek&t=18s (Elementary School)
https://www.youtube.com/watch?v=02bN4JFx10Y (Middle/High School)

Process Question:
In what ways did utilizing the Emotion Freedom Technique enable you to relieve your stress and experience calmness?

Creative Activity 1
In N' Out of Control: Have students record five things in their lives that they have control over and have students record five things in their lives that they do NOT have control over.

Upon completion process:
What relationship exists between control and anxiety?
Discuss the importance of accepting what we cannot change and changing what we can in order to reduce anxiety...
Indicate steps that you can take to further enhance control over things in your life that you can change....

Creative Activity 2
Color Me Free of Anxiety: Students will draw a picture of what anxiety represents to them, as well as name their image in order to separate a person from the problem and externalize/release their anxiety.

Discussion Questions:
In what ways did this activity enable you to experience less anxiety?
How is drawing and naming your anxiety beneficial?
What are some additional steps you can take to experience reduced anxiety?

Feedback:
Counselors can either ask for verbal or written feedback in order to assess the impact of a session on student outcomes:
On a scale from one to five (1 being low and 5 being high) rate the following:

- This session helped to raise my awareness about anxiety.

- This session helped me to recognize the impact anxiety has on me academically, socially, and emotionally.
- This session provided me with tools I can use to better manage my anxiety.
- This session helped me to feel more in control and less anxious.

Lesson Plan 2: Depression

Directions: This activity can be facilitated in a classroom, small group, or individual counseling setting. First, the definition of depression will be addressed. Students will then process open-ended questions, complete the evidence-based practice activity, the creative activity, follow-up discussion questions in order to review material learned, as well as feedback questions to assess the impact of the session on student learning outcomes.

Definition of Depression: Depression is a mental health issue that impacts the way people think, feel, and act. Depression may cause feelings of sadness or loss of interest in things someone once enjoyed. It can also involve having a change in appetite, sleeping habits, and having a loss of energy.

Open-Ended Questions:
What words do you think of when you hear the word depression?
Sadness/feeling down/alone
Discuss some causes of feelings of sadness...
Family/friends/school
In what ways does depression impact our emotions, social skills, and academics?
Negative impact on feelings, relationships, academic performance.
Share the importance of talking to someone if you are feeling sad...
So we feel supported and less alone.
What are some strategies that you can use to feel better if you are feeling down?
Talking, journaling, writing

Evidence-Based Practice Activity 1: PHQ-9 in order to obtain a baseline measure of the level of students' depression https://med.stanford.edu/fastlab/research/imapp/msrs/_jcr_content/main/accordion/accordion_content3/download_256324296/file.res/PHQ9%20id%20date%2008.03.pdf

Evidence-Based Practice Activity 2: Exception Find Question
Ask each student participant to answer the following: A time in my life when I did not feel sad/down was....
It is important to identify times when the challenge did not exist in order to build on previous successes.

Creative Activity 1: My Utopia

- Ask students to close their eyes and think of a place in their mind that brings them a sense of peace and utopia.
- Ask students to think about the colors, images, and people they see and sounds they hear.
- Have students draw the image that reflects their utopia.

Creative Activity 2: Cup O' Gratitude

- Each student will have a plastic cup, Sharpee Markers, and popsicle sticks.
- Students can decorate the outside of their plastic cups with words and images that reflect gratitude.
- On popsicle sticks, students can record things in their life that they are grateful for/appreciative of, as this helps to foster feelings of joy and hope.

Discussion Questions

What is the importance of envisioning your utopia image in your mind if you are feeling down/sad?

In what ways is it important to process things in our lives that we are grateful for in order to reduce feelings of sadness?

What would need to occur in order for you to feel more happiness?

As happiness is a choice, what is one thing you can do in your life to experience greater joy?

Feedback:

Counselors can either ask for verbal or written feedback in order to assess the impact of the session on student outcomes:

On a scale from one to five (1 being low and 5 being high) rate the following:

- This session helped to raise my awareness about depression.
- This session helped me to recognize the impact depression has on me academically, socially, and emotionally.
- This session provided me with tools I can use to better manage feelings associated with depression.
- This session helped me to feel happier and more hopeful.

Lesson Plan 3: Self-esteem

Directions: This activity can be facilitated in a classroom, small group, or individual counseling setting. First, the definition of self-esteem will be addressed. Students will then process open-ended questions, complete the evidence-based practice activity, the creative activity, follow-up discussion

questions in order to review material learned, as well as feedback questions to assess the impact of the session on student learning outcomes.

Definition of Self-esteem: Confidence in one's own abilities and demonstrating self-respect. Feeling good about oneself and one's choices/accomplishments.

Open-Ended Questions:
What words come to mind when you think about self-esteem?
Self-worth, self-concept
Discuss the impact that media and peers have on our self-esteem...
Directly that influences the way we feel about ourselves.
In what ways does self-esteem impact academic performance, social skills, and behaviors?
Low self-worth has negative impact on academic performance, social skills, and behaviors.
What is the importance of developing a healthy and positive self-esteem/self-concept?
This allows us to believe in ourselves and achieve our goals and dreams.

Evidence-Based Practice: Rosenberg self-esteem scale in order to obtain a baseline measure of students' self-esteem
https://fetzer.org/sites/default/files/images/stories/pdf/selfmeasures/Self_Measures_for_Self-Esteem_ROSENBERG_SELF-ESTEEM.pdf

Creative Activity: I Love Me Electronic Collage

- Students will use their laptops/Chrome Books/iPads to create an I Love Me Collage.
- Students will find pictures, images, inspirational quotes, phrases, shapes that showcase their strengths, inner resources, and love for themselves.
- Students will use colors and fonts that reflect their personality and positive attributes.
- Students can include their favorite foods, hobbies, and passions.

The purpose of this activity is for students to reflect upon the many strengths, talents, and gifts that students possess and to celebrate them in an innovative and inspiring way.

Discussion Questions:
In what ways does self-esteem allow us to create an accepting, safe, and inclusive school climate?
How did this activity enable you to augment and showcase your self-esteem?
What is the importance of developing a strong self-concept?

In what ways does having high self-esteem motivate us to reach our fullest potential?

Share steps that you can take to show yourselves more compassion and self-love…

Feedback:

Counselors can either ask for verbal or written feedback in order to assess the impact of the session on student outcomes:

On a scale from one to five (1 being low and 5 being high) rate the following:
This session helped to raise my awareness about self-esteem.

This session helped me to recognize the impact that self-esteem has on my academic performance, choices, and interpersonal relationships.

This session helped me to recognize steps that I can take in order to amplify my self-esteem.

This session enabled me to recognize the significance of possessing high self-esteem.

Lesson Plan 4: Optimism and Hope

Directions: This activity can be facilitated in a classroom, small group, or individual counseling setting. First, the definition of optimism and hope will be addressed. Students will then process open-ended questions, complete the evidence-based practice activity, the creative activity, follow-up discussion questions in order to review material learned, as well as feedback questions to assess the impact of a session on student learning outcomes.

Definition of Optimism and Hope: Optimism is hopefulness and confidence about the future or a successful outcome of something. Hope is the expectation/wish of something that is desired.

Open-Ended Questions:

When you think of optimism and hope, what adjectives come to mind?
Positivity, belief, resilience
Discuss the importance of demonstrating optimism and positivity…
This enhances our motivation to move forward in a positive direction
What is the importance of having a growth mindset?
Knowledge and learning is not fixed and can grow if given the opportunity and resources
What relationship exists between optimism and hope and reducing bullying/ school violence?
When students are hopeful and positive, they are less likely to attack others and are more focused on promoting well-being and safety for all.
Share the types of characteristics optimistic and hopeful people possess…
Positive, upbeat, charismatic, strength-based, future-focused

Evidence-Based Practice 1: Life Orientation Test (LOT-R) in order to obtain a baseline measure of students' level of optimism and hope https://fetzer.org/sites/default/files/images/stories/pdf/selfmeasures/Self_Measures_for_Love_and_Compassion_Research_OPTIMISM.pdf

Evidence-Based Practice 2: Growth Mindset Positive Self-Statements

- Students will record three criticisms that they say about themselves.
- Using a growth mindset, students will reframe these negative criticisms into positive statements that boost optimism, motivation, and hope.
- Negative Statement: I will never be good at anything.
- Growth Mindset Positive Self-Statement: I may not understand this **YET**, but if I keep working at it, eventually I will master this.

Notice that by emphasizing, "yet" this allows students to understand that there are endless opportunities for growth, as nothing is finite. Modifying self-sabotaging statements into growth mindset statements is very powerful and integral for enhancing optimism, hope, and drive to move forward.

Creative Activity: Reach For The Stars

- Counselors will provide black construction paper, Sharpie markers, white chalk, and cutouts of large yellow star shapes for students.
- Students will then glue or tape their large yellow star to the black construction paper in order to create an illusion of outer space.
- On the star, students will illustrate an image of how they envision themselves in the future.
- Next to their star, students will use white chalk to record hopes and dreams they have for themselves personally and professionally and steps that they can take to maintain optimism and make these come to fruition.

Discussion Questions:
In what ways do optimism and hope allow us to create a safe, collaborative, and uplifting school climate?
How did this activity help you to become mindful of the importance of demonstrating optimism and hope?
What is the importance of being optimistic and hopeful, especially when facing challenges?
How does having a growth mindset enable us to be more positive and optimistic?
What strategies can we use to create more magic, hope, and optimism, in our lives?

Feedback:
Counselors can either ask for verbal or written feedback in order to assess the impact of the session on student outcomes:
On a scale from one to five (1 being low and 5 being high) rate the following:
This session helped to raise my awareness about optimism and hope.
This session helped me to recognize the impact that optimism and hope have on my academic performance and goal attainment.
This session helped me to recognize steps that I can take in order to amplify my optimism and hope.
This session enabled me to recognize the significance of possessing a high degree of optimism and hope for my present and future in order to be the best that I can be.

Elementary/Primary Activities to Become My Best SELf

Lesson 1: Identifying Strengths

Lesson Plan Objective: To help students understand the importance of identifying inner strengths/resources in order to reach their fullest potential.

Materials: Markers, Paper, Magazines, Art Supplies

Group Questions:

1 **Ask students what do the words strength/inner resources mean?**
   Identifying attributes, strengths, talents, and gifts that we innately possess within ourselves.
2 **Ask students what is the importance of identifying strengths/inner resources?**
   To be mindful of areas that we excel in, as well as be able to set and achieve academic/behavioral/social goals based upon our attributes and abilities.
3 **What tools can we use to help us identify our strengths?**

Our accomplishments, achievements, feedback from parents, friends, teachers, and counselors.

Activity 1: "You" nique You
Students will individually record responses and debrief their peers about what makes them unique ☺.

• Things that they are good at
• Accolades/praise they have received
• What they like most about their personality
• Struggles they have overcome

- Ways they have assisted others
- Three traits that make them special
- Top three values
- What happiness means to them
- What they need to be happy/fulfilled

Activity 2: I Am Poster
Stakeholders will assist students in making "I Am Poster." "I Am Posters" will highlight each student's unique and special qualities, mannerisms, and foibles; ultimately representing one's authentic self and what makes them so exceptional. Students will write "I Am" in the middle of their poster. Students will then decorate the poster with words, adjectives, images, colors, and quotes that represent their self-concept, as well as identify their strengths, inner resources, and positive attributes. Upon completion, students can share their masterpieces with their class and hang up their "I Am Poster" on the wall in order to remind themselves to always celebrate their unique qualities.

Follow-Up Questions:
What is the importance of identifying one's strengths?
Discuss the significance of having a positive self-concept…
What are some ways we can remind ourselves of our special qualities?

Group Feedback:
I enjoyed today's activity? ☺ or ☹
This activity helped me to identify and recognize my strengths. ☺ or ☹
This activity helped me to understand the importance of having a positive self-concept. ☺ or ☹

Lesson 2: Growth Mindset

Lesson Plan Objective: To help students understand the importance of possessing a growth mindset, to recognize that intelligence is not a fixed trait and that growth is possible via exposure, experience, optimism, and opportunity to apply and practice the knowledge obtained.

Materials: Markers, Paper

Group Questions:

1 **Ask students whether they believe intelligence is a fixed trait…**
   Intelligence is not a fixed trait and can be enhanced and improved via exposure, experiences, practice, and opportunities with resources.
2 **Discuss the importance of having a growth mindset?**
   People who believe that intelligence and growth can be increased are more likely to persevere, work harder, and seek to master skills.
3 **What steps can we take to promote a growth mindset?**

Engage in reflective practice by identifying strengths and areas needed to improve, utilize positive reframes, and engage in positive self-talk.

Activity 1: Putting a Positive Spin ☺

Using the template below, students will individually record responses and provide positive reframes using a Growth Mindset to the following and debrief in a large group upon completion ☺. When reframing using a Growth Mindset, it is vital to use the word YET, as we are constantly working toward self-actualization and becoming the best we can be

Example: Negative Statement: I will never reach my goal.
Positive Reframe: "Even though I haven't achieved it YET, I will work hard until I do."

I'm not good at this.

_____
_____
_____

I give up.

_____
_____
_____

This is too hard.

_____
_____
_____

I made a mistake.

_____
_____
_____

I'm not smart enough.

_____
_____
_____

Activity 2: Super Selfie

Stakeholders will assist students in making "Super Selfies." Students will draw a caricature of their super selves on the template below.

Super Self-Caricature:

"I believe in my #selfie by....

_____

My goal this year is to...

_____

I can...

_____

I cannot...yet, but with practice, I will improve!

One mistake I have made

What I have learned about myself as a result of making those mistakes

---

If I think, believe, and dare to dream big, I will...

Follow-Up Questions:
What is the importance of possessing a growth mindset?
In what ways is it essential to persevere in school and life...
Discuss the significance of making mistakes and learning from our mistakes...

Group Feedback:
I enjoyed today's activity? ☺ or ☹
This activity helped me to identify and recognize my strengths and areas for growth. ☺ or ☹
This activity helped me to understand the importance of having a growth mindset. ☺ or ☹

Lesson 3: Goal Setting

Lesson Plan Objective: To help students understand the importance of identifying inner strengths and building upon strengths in order to achieve specific, measurable, achievable, realistic, and timely (SMART) goals

Materials: Markers, Paper, Magazines, and Scissors

Group Questions:

1   **Ask students what does the word "goal"mean?**
    A target that someone works toward achieving
2   **Ask students what is the importance of goal setting?**
    Goals provide direction, motivation, and inspiration and help us work toward achieving our dreams
3   **What are some steps we can take to set strength-based goals?**

    •   First, we need to identify our strengths.
    •   Second, we need to determine what it is we want to achieve/work toward.
    •   Third, we need to determine how we can build upon our strengths to achieve our goals.
    •   Fourth, record our goals to monitor and keep track of our progress toward achievement.

Activity 1: READY, SET, GOals
Using the template below, students will individually record FIVE goals that they would like to achieve this school year, indicate which strength they will utilize to achieve their S.M.A.R.T. goal, as well as steps that need to be taken to achieve their goals

Goal 1_____ Strength:_____
Steps to Achieve Goal: _____
Goal 2_____ Strength:_____
Steps to Achieve Goal: _____
Goal 3_____ Strength:_____
Steps to Achieve Goal: _____
Goal 4_____ Strength:_____
Steps to Achieve Goal: _____
Goal 5_____ Strength:_____
Steps to Achieve Goal: _____

Activity 2 Vision Board:
Stakeholders will assist students in making vision boards based upon their identified goals. A vision board enables students to visualize their future goal, prompting them to work toward achieving the same. The vision board reflects the mantra of seeing → believing → achieving. When students are able to see their goals, they will then be more likely to take steps to achieve these goals and make them come to fruition. Students will use construction paper, markers, magazine cutouts, sparkles, words, pictures, and quotes that illustrate and represent their goals. Upon completion, students will be encouraged to leave their vision boards in their bedroom at home so that they are consistently reminded of what their goals are and what steps need to be taken to achieve their goals.

Follow-Up Questions:
What is the importance of setting strength-based goals?
Discuss the significance of using a vision board to illustrate our goals...
What is the importance of working diligently to achieve our goals in life?

Group Feedback:
I enjoyed today's activity? ☺ or ☹
This activity helped me to identify and set strength-based goals. ☺ or ☹
This activity helped me to understand the importance of visualizing goals in order to achieve them. ☺ or ☹

Lesson 4: Negative Self-Talk

Lesson Plan Objective: To help students understand the definition of negative self-talk, the detrimental impact negative self-talk has on our self-concept, as well as the importance of saying positive affirmations each day based on our intrinsic qualities and strengths in order to boost our self-concept and mindset.

Materials: Markers, Paper, Oscar the Grouch/Cookie Monster Stuffed Animals

Group Questions:

1 **Ask students what does negative self-talk refers to?**
   Saying negative criticisms/statements about oneself that impedes one's ability to self-actualize and grow.
2 **Discuss some consequences of negative self-talk...**
   Feelings of inferiority, failure, poor self-worth, low self-esteem, self-defeating thoughts, anxiety, depression, self-harm.
3 **What are some steps we can take to change our negative self-talk into positive self-talk?**
   Thought stopping (as soon as a negative thought appears, stop this thought and modify the thought into a more positive statement); **reframing** (turning negatives into positives); **identifying the silver lining** (what we learn and as a result how we became stronger); **saying positive affirmations** every day in the morning in the mirror. Positive affirmations should be based on one's intrinsic strengths and need to be stated repeatedly. Starting the day out in a positive mindset helps to build resilience and promotes optimism and leads to a self-fulfilling prophecy (LeMouse, 2018).
4 **Indicate the importance of identifying one's strengths and their relationship with positive self-talk**
   We become more self-aware, able to focus on our inner resources, experience a sense of pride and accomplishment, hope, control, and empowered feelings. When people feel a sense of pride and worthiness, they feel validated and engage in more positive self-talk, leading to greater productivity, efficiency, and enhanced self-worth

Activity 1: Super Me Activity

Stakeholders will assist students in recording their responses to the following statements using the template below. Upon completion, students will share their responses with their peers.

Indicate your super strengths.

_____

_____

_____

Describe your authentic super self (the way you see yourself through your own eyes, rather than the way you would like others to see you).

_____

_____

_____

Discuss what you need in your life to be truly happy (what can you not live without?).

_____

_____

_____

One trait I love most about myself that makes me SUPER.

_____

_____

_____

Activity 2: Don't Judge Me. Love Me. Activity

Stakeholders will discuss and define what an internal judger means. An internal judger is a voice/image/picture that comes to mind when people say negative/hurtful/defeating comments about themselves. Drawing an internal judger is important, as this helps to externalize rather than internalize these negative statements separating a person from the problem. Using the template below, complete the following:

Example: Negative Criticism: No one likes me.
Positive Reframe: I love me.

Draw your internal judger and name your internal judger on a **separate** piece of paper.

Record three main criticisms you say about yourself.

1
2
3

Indicate how your criticisms have impacted your self-worth.

_____

_____

_____

Record positive reframes to each of the criticisms recorded.

1
2
3

Discuss the steps that you can take to become less self-critical and more accepting.

1

2

3

Upon completion, students will share their responses. Students will first share their negative criticisms and will then share their positive reframes.

Follow-Up Questions:
What is the importance of engaging in positive self-talk?
Discuss consequences of engaging in negative self-talk...
Indicate the importance of positively reframing negative thoughts...

Group Feedback:
I enjoyed today's activity? ☺ or ☹
This activity helped me to reframe negative into positive thoughts. ☺ or ☹
This activity helped me to feel more empowered and accepting of myself.
☺ or ☹

Lesson 5: Empowerment

Lesson Plan Objective: To educate students about the definition of empowerment, as well as the importance of experiencing feelings of empowerment in order to work toward self-actualization.

Materials: Markers, Paper

Group Questions:

1   **Ask students what does the word empowerment means?**
     Feeling able, capable, competent, self-assured, self-confident, and in control
2   **Discuss some ways people can experience feelings of empowerment...**
     Setting and achieving goals, stating positive affirmations, identifying and recognizing strengths, and focusing on what one can control.
3   **What is the importance of feeling empowered?**
     Recognize that in life we only fail when we stop trying, more motivated, inspired, driven, and focused on achieving strength-based goals, as well as enhanced feelings of self-control.

Activity 1: Control Activity
Using the template below, stakeholders will assist students in recording their responses to the following statements. Upon completion, students will share their responses with their peers

Indicate five aspects of your life that you DO have control over.

1
2
3
4
5

Indicate five aspects of your life that you DO NOT have control over.

1
2
3
4
5

Record the steps you can take to experience greater control over the things you listed that you can control.

1
2
3
4
5

Activity 2: Challenges to Successes
Stakeholders will assist students in recording their responses to the following using the template below:
Discuss a time in your life when you did not achieve a goal you set.

_____
_____
_____

What emotions did you experience?

_____
_____
_____

What did you learn about yourself as a result of going through this experience?

_____
_____
_____

Looking at this experience through a more positive lens, how can this challenging life experience now be seen as a success and triumph?

_____
_____
_____

Think about a time when you felt empowered in your life. How did you feel and what can you do in the future to feel empowered again?

_____
_____

Follow-Up Questions:
What is the importance of experiencing feelings of empowerment?
What are some ways in which we can feel empowered?
Indicate the importance of focusing on what we can control instead of what is out of our control...

Group Feedback:
I enjoyed today's activity? ☺ or ☹
This activity helped me to understand the importance of focusing on what I can control in my life. ☺ or ☹
This activity helped me to feel more empowered and instilled a sense of hope. ☺ or ☹

Lesson 6: Self-Acceptance

Lesson Plan Objective: To educate students about the importance of self-acceptance in order to experience feelings of fulfillment, appreciation, gratitude, self-love, and work toward reaching one's fullest potential.

Materials: Markers, Paper, Pasta, Scissors, and Aluminum Foil

Group Questions:

1   **Ask students what does the word self-acceptance means?**
    Accepting one's qualities, flaws, attributes, mannerisms, and foibles, as these qualities are what make us each unique and special.
2   **Discuss the importance of self-acceptance.**
    Self-acceptance allows self-forgiveness, feelings of peace, serenity, fulfillment, integration, wholeness, celebration, and gratitude for one's individuality.
3   **In what ways does the idea of perfection relate to self-acceptance?**
    Perfection is an ideal that does not exist. Our flaws are what makes us exceptional. In order to experience self-acceptance, we need to embrace our authentic selves (faults and all). Perfection impedes self-acceptance, as those striving for perfection are attempting to achieve goals that are not realistic or feasible.

4   **What are some steps we can take to become more self-accepting and demonstrate greater self-love?**
Stop being so critical/judgmental, do not compare ourselves to others, celebrate all of our unique qualities, focus on our positive attributes, demonstrate self-forgiveness, and engage in self-care.

Activity 1: Mirror Me Activity
Stakeholders will assist students in creating mirrors using popsicle sticks, sticky jewels, aluminum foil, and construction paper. Upon completion, students will look into their mirror and state responses for the following:

What does the word perfection mean?

_____

_____

How has the idea of perfection impacted how you feel about yourself?

_____

_____

What attributes do you love most about yourself?

_____

_____

Who is your hero and what have you learned from them?

_____

_____

What can you do to be less critical and more accepting of yourself?

_____

_____

_____

Activity 2: I Love Pasta and Me Activity
Explain the following: The relationship we have with ourselves is the most important relationship that we experience in our lifetime. Self-love is important as it allows us to accept, forgive, and cherish ourselves always. Despite some mistakes we have made, self-love enables us to recognize these experiences as teachable moments and we are able to learn, grow, and become better as a result. Stakeholders will assist students in completing the following using the template below:

Describe a situation/example when you demonstrated self-love

_____

_____

_____

Five things that you love about yourself and your life.

1

2

3

4

5

What do you do to show your self-love?

_____

_____

_____

What are some things that you can do to love yourself more?

_____

_____

_____

Using pasta, sculpt what self-love looks like to you...

Follow-Up Questions:
What does self-acceptance mean?
What are some ways in which we can demonstrate self-acceptance and self-love?
Indicate the importance of experiencing self-acceptance and self-love...

Group Feedback:
I enjoyed today's activity? ☺ or ☹
This activity helped me to understand the importance of self-acceptance. ☺ or ☹
This activity helped me to feel more accepting of myself. ☺ or ☹

References

Bandura, A., Barbaranelli, C., Caprara, G. V., & Pastorelli, C. (2001). Self-efficacy beliefs as shapers of children's aspirations and career trajectories. *Child Development*, *72(1)*, 187–206. Retrieved from http://www.uky.edu/~eushe2/Bandura/Bandura2001CD.pdf

LeMouse, M. (2018). Positive thinking and positive affirmations for a successful life. Retrieved from https://www.healthguidance.org/entry/11743/1/Positive-Thinking-and-Positive-Affirmations-for-a-Successful-Life.html

Mayer, J. D., Salovey, P., & Caruso, D. R. (2004). Emotional intelligence: Theory, findings, and implications. *Psychological Inquiry*, *15(3)*, 197–215.

Weissberg, R. (2016). Why social and emotional learning is essential for students. Retrieved from https://www.edutopia.org/blog/why-sel-essential-for-students-weissberg-durlak-domitrovich-gullotta

16 Self-Management

Self-management is being able to regulate one's emotions, handle stress, control impulses, and delay gratification (Weissberg, 2016). Self-management is a critical skill to possess, as it enables people to persevere, work to overcome challenges, as well as manage emotions in an appropriate way (Gullone, Hughes, King, & Tonge, 2010). Students who possess this skill are better able to cope with stress, manage their emotions, and have been found to experience an easier transition to college, as well as achieve higher academic performance. in comparison to peers who lack this skill (DeBerard, Speilmans, & Julka, 2004).

Secondary Activities

Lesson Plan 1: Emotion Regulation

Directions: This activity can be facilitated in a classroom, small group, or individual counseling setting. First, the definition of emotion regulation will be addressed. Students will then process open-ended questions, complete the evidence-based practice activity, the creative activity, follow-up discussion questions in order to review material learned, as well as feedback questions to assess the impact of session on student learning outcomes.

Definition of Emotion Regulation: A person's ability to regulate their emotions and demonstrate self-control.

Open-Ended Questions:
What does emotion regulation entail?
Stay in control of emotions and demonstrate restraint
How does emotion regulation help us to have more control over our behaviors?
Demonstrating emotion regulation allows us to think before acting and consider the consequences of actions.

DOI: 10.4324/9781003262183-16

In what ways does emotion regulation enable us to be more successful academically?
We are more focused, structured, organized, and attentive.
What are some strategies you currently use to engage in self-control?
Deep breathing, counting, drawing, mindfulness
Evidence-Based Practice Activity 1: Mindfulness
https://www.youtube.com/watch?v=wf5K3pP2IUQ **(Elementary School)**
https://www.youtube.com/watch?v=HvWGO3iQNiU **(Middle & High School)**
Mindfulness is an empirically based practice that is shown to help people feel grounded, more in control, and centered, which is vital for emotion regulation

Evidence-Based Practice Activity 2: Logical Consequences
- Ask students to think of a choice that they need to make.
- Ask students to each record the following prompt: Tell me what will happen if you do this and tell me what will happen if you do NOT do this …
- Have students record their responses in order to make the most thoughtful and informed choice, as this teaches students to think before acting.

Having students engage in logical consequences is important for emotion regulation, as it allows them to process the pros and cons of a choice before acting and reduces impulsivity

Creative Activity A: Mold My Best Self
- Using Play-Doh students will mold themselves demonstrating self-control.
- Students can mold themselves figuratively or literally.
- Students will present their clay masterpieces with one another upon completion, as well as process how the activity helped motivate them to demonstrate greater self-control.

Creative Activity B: Sparkle N' Shine Bottle
- Using a water bottle, warm glue, and glitter, students will make a Sparkle N' Shine Bottle.
- Students can use colors of glitter that reflect calmness and peace.
- As students shake the bottle, the floating flitter represents chaos and loss of control, but as the glitter settles this reflects serenity, control, and tranquility.
- Students can use their Sparkle N' Shine Bottle at their desks or at home when feeling agitated in order to regain control and restore calmness.

Discussion Questions

In what ways is visualizing an image of yourself demonstrating self-control important?

In what ways do these activities help you to better regulate your emotions and demonstrate restraint?

What is the importance of emotion regulation?

How does emotion regulation help us to be more successful in school and in life?

What steps can you take to further enhance your emotion regulation skills?

Feedback:

Counselors can either ask for verbal or written feedback in order to assess for impact of the session on student outcomes:

On a scale from one to five (1 being low and 5 being high) rate the following:

- This session helped to raise my awareness about emotion regulation.
- This session helped me to recognize the impact emotion regulation has on me academically, socially, and emotionally.
- This session provided me with tools I can use to better manage my emotion regulation.
- This session helped me to feel more grounded, focused, and in control.

Lesson Plan 2: Motivation

Directions: This activity can be facilitated in a classroom, small group, or individual counseling setting. First, the definition of motivation will be addressed. Students will then process open-ended questions, complete the evidence-based practice activity, the creative activity, follow-up discussion questions in order to review material learned, as well as feedback questions to assess the impact of the session on student learning outcomes.

Definition of Motivation: The reason or reasons one has for acting or behaving in a certain way.

Discussion Questions:

What does motivation mean to you?

Motivation means one's ability and desire to achieve goals

Discuss the importance of having a high degree of intrinsic motivation?

Motivation allows us to envision goals we want to achieve, as well as determine steps we need to take to accomplish these goals.

In what ways does motivation enable us to be successful in school and life?

The more motivated and driven we are, the more likely we will be to achieve goals.

Greatest sources of motivation in my life include ...

Family, school, myself, peers

Possessing motivation can help to reduce bullying and aggression by ...
The more motivated one is to achieve, the less likely one will be to lash out aggressively at others, as empathy and compassion are necessary for success.

Evidence-Based Practice: Set, Believe, Achieve

• Students will identify three SMART goals that they want to set that align with their inner resources and strengths.
• Students will break down these larger and identify steps that need to be taken in order to achieve their main goal in due time.

Goal setting is a wonderful strategy to use to enhance intrinsic motivation, as doing so promotes focus, direction, and inspiration to achieve greatness.

Creative Activity: Nothing Can Stop Me Now
Using construction paper, stakeholders will distribute a large pre-cutout of an image of a black stoplight with a red/yellow/green circle to students.

• Students will then individually record using white chalk three challenges that they face that are impeding upon them from achieving their goals and record these challenges around the red circle on the stoplight.
• Students will then record three traits using white chalk that they possess that will help them to achieve their goals (despite these challenges) and record these traits around the yellow circle on the stoplight.
• Students will then record three steps using white chalk that they can take to overcome challenges and achieve their goals and record these steps around the green circle on the stoplight.

Upon completion, hang up the stoplight in the classroom or in the counselor's office to remind students of their abilities and continuously motivate them to achieve excellence.

Discussion Questions:
Discuss the importance of motivation in regard to promoting inclusivity and security in school and the workplace ...
In what ways did these activities enable you to enhance your intrinsic motivation?
How does setting goals help to increase one's motivation?
What emotions do you experience when you achieve a goal?
What can you do in order to augment your level and others' levels of motivation?

Feedback:
Counselors can either ask for verbal or written feedback in order to assess for impact of the session on student outcomes:
On a scale from one to five (1 being low and 5 being high) rate the following:

- This session helped to raise my awareness about motivation.
- This session helped me to recognize the impact that motivation has on my academic performance, emotions, and behaviors.
- This session helped me to recognize the steps I need to take in order to amplify my motivation.
- This session provided me with tools I can use to enhance my motivation.
- This session helped me to become more cognizant of the importance of motivation in order to have a safer and more secure school climate, as well as a productive and efficient workforce.

Lesson Plan 3: Stress Management

Directions: This activity can be facilitated in a classroom, small group, or individual counseling setting. First, the definition of stress management will be addressed. Students will then process open-ended questions, complete the evidence-based practice activity, the creative activity, follow-up discussion questions in order to review material learned, as well as feedback questions to assess the impact of the session on student learning outcomes

Definition of Stress Management: Includes a range of strategies that can be used to help people better manage stress in order to live happier, healthier, and more fulfilling lives. Learning problem-solving skills, enhancing coping skills, practicing relaxation tactics, and improving relationships help to enhance stress management.

Open-Ended Questions:

How would you describe stress?
Challenges, feeling overwhelmed, having many responsibilities
Discuss triggers of stress in your life …
School, work, friends, relationships, family
What is the importance of managing stress?
Managing stress is important so that we do not burn out and become ill.
What are some academic, social, and emotional consequences people face if stress is not managed effectively?
Decreased performance, feeling isolated, feeling sad and angry.
How does managing stress help us to reduce aggression?
Managing stress allows people to feel more in control of their emotions and empowered.
Evidence-Based Practice: Student Stress Survey in order to obtain a baseline measure of the degree to which students experience stress at

school and at home http://wp.lps.org/dclarid/files/2012/08/Student-Stress-Survey.pdf

Creative Activity: Essential Oils Stress Ball
Students will need a balloon, flour, funnel, Sharpie marker, and scented oil (peppermint or lavender) to complete the activity.

- Students will fill a balloon up with flour.
- On their filled balloon, students will use a Sharpie marker and record words/images/shapes on the balloon that represent relaxation, calmness, and de-stressing.
- Students will add a few drops of scented oil inside of their balloon in order to enhance and promote relaxation.
- Students can squeeze their stress ball at school or home in order to release and better manage their stress.

Discussion Questions:
In wht ways does managing stress help to foster a safer, happier, and healthier school climate?
In what ways did these activities raise your awareness about the importance of stress management?
What coping skills/strategies are helpful in mitigating stress?
Indicate the steps that you can take to further improve your stress management skills in order to be more successful in school and in the workforce ...

Feedback:
Counselors can either ask for verbal or written feedback in order to assess the impact of the session on student outcomes:
On a scale from one to five (1 being low and 5 being high) rate the following:

- This session helped to raise my awareness about stress management.
- This session helped me to recognize the impact that stress management has on my academic performance, emotions, and behaviors.
- This session helped me to recognize the coping skills and strategies I can use in order to amplify my stress management skills.
- This session provided me with tools I can use to enhance my stress management.
- This session helped me to become more mindful of the importance of stress management in order to have a safer and healthier school climate, as well as a calmer and more focused workforce.

Lesson Plan 4: Anger Management

Directions: This activity can be facilitated in a classroom, small group, or individual counseling setting. First, the definition of anger management will

be addressed. Students will then process open-ended questions, complete the evidence-based practice activity, the creative activity, follow-up discussion questions in order to review material learned, as well as feedback questions to assess the impact of the session on student learning outcomes.

Definition of Anger Management: Process of recognizing signs that one is becoming angry and being able to take action to calm down and cope in a healthy way before the anger escalates or intensifies.

Open-Ended Questions:

Share words to describe anger …
Upset, mad, frustrated
What are some consequences of displaying anger in a destructive way?
Leads to behavioral issues, loss of friends, truancy
In what ways does anger impact our mental health?
Anger can lead to increased feelings of anger and depression if internalized.
Discuss the importance of managing our anger in constructive ways …
We are able to express our frustration in ways that are proactive rather than reactive; allowing us to experience greater self-control.
What type of relationship exists between anger and bullying/school violence?
Typically, the angrier one is, the more likely that person may be to engage in bullying or carry out acts of violence.

Evidence-Based Practice Activity: Triggers of Anger
- Students can individually record five topics that trigger levels of anger.
- Students will then individually read aloud each of their triggers and in a group, process healthy ways to deal with triggers when faced with them.

Creative Activity: Anger Animal
- Students will draw an image of an animal that they believe reflects anger.
- The animal can be literal or figurative in nature.
- Students will use images, shapes, and colors that epitomize anger.
- Students will name their animal as a way to identify anger.
- Surrounding their image students will record:

  - The way their body feels when they get angry.
  - Emotions they experience when angry.
  - Current ways of coping/managing anger.

- Upon completion, students will present their anger animals and in a group students and counselor will process healthy strategies students can use to de-escalate anger before it intensifies

  - Mindfulness, counting, deep breathing, walking away, writing, talking

Discussion Questions

In what ways does managing our anger allow us to perform better academically, behaviorally, and socially?

Discuss the importance of managing our anger in healthy ways ...

In what ways did this activity enable you to process and release feelings associated with anger?

What steps can you take in the future to further enhance your anger management skills?

Feedback:

Counselors can either ask for verbal or written feedback in order to assess the impact of the session on student outcomes:

On a scale from one to five (1 being low and 5 being high) rate the following:

- This session helped to raise my awareness about anger management.
- This session helped me to recognize the impact that anger has on my academic performance, emotions, and behaviors.
- This session helped me to recognize the coping skills and strategies I can use in order to amplify my anger management skills.
- This session enabled me to mitigate my anger.

Lesson Plan 5: Grief and Loss

Directions: This activity can be facilitated in a classroom, small group, or individual counseling setting. First, the definition of grief and loss will be addressed. Students will then process open-ended questions, complete the evidence-based practice activity, the creative activity, follow-up discussion questions in order to review material learned, as well as feedback questions to assess the impact of the session on student learning outcomes.

Definition of Grief and Loss: Grief is the natural response to loss; the loss of a loved one, an animal, a relationship. Grief is characterized by deep sadness due to loss in life.

Open-Ended Questions:

How would you describe grief and loss?
Sadness, anger, devastation, heartbreak

If grief were an image, what would it look like to you?
A dark cloud

In what ways do grief and loss impact our academic performance, behaviors, and social skills?
Negative impact on academic performance, behaviors, and social skills. People may isolate themselves or act out if feeling sad.

Describe the relationship that exists between grief and loss and bullying/ school violence ...

There is a direct relationship between grief and loss and bullying/school violence. Those struggling with grief and loss and are experiencing anger and loss of hope may engage in unhealthy behaviors.

Evidence-Based Practice: Talk to the Chair
- Using the Empty Chair Technique, students can complete this activity as a role play in front of their peers or each student can complete the activity individually.
- Students will talk to a chair and share with the chair everything that they wanted to say, but never had a chance to say to the person/ relationship that they lost.
- Students are encouraged to convey emotions experienced, as well as the challenges of navigating their new normal without this person/ relationship.
- Using the Empty Chair Technique can be a powerful medium to use in order to release internalized grief and sadness in order to begin the process of healing.

Creative Activity: Memory Time Capsule
- Students will use a shoebox or plastic Tupperware; either one from home or one that is supplied to them.
- Students will decorate the outside of their boxes with words, images, shapes, and quotes that reflect their relationship and love for the person whom they lost.
- Inside of the box, students can place items, photographs, letters, cards, memorabilia, or gifts that remind them of the person.
- Upon completion, students will process steps that they can take to continue celebrating and carrying on the person's legacy.
- Students can open their Memory Time Capsule anytime they are feeling sad or alone in order to feel more connected and bonded to their loved one.

Discussion Questions:

In what ways do grief and loss profoundly impact us in school and in life?

How do addressing grief and loss help us to create a safer and more inclusive school climate?

What are some healthy coping skills we can use to process our grief and sadness?

Share the importance of talking about our grief and loss when we are ready rather than internalizing it ...

In what ways did this activity allow you to process feelings of grief?

What steps can you take moving forward in order to continue to heal?

Lesson Plan 6: Resilience

Directions: This activity can be facilitated in a classroom, small group, or individual counseling setting. First, the definition of resilience will be addressed. Students will then process open-ended questions, complete the evidence-based practice activity, the creative activity, follow-up discussion questions in order to review material learned, as well as feedback questions to assess the impact of the session on student learning outcomes.

Definition of Resilience: The capacity to recover quickly and to overcome adversity; not allowing challenges to prevent us from reaching our fullest potential

Open-Ended Questions:

What does the phrase, "You never fail until you stop trying," mean to you?
People never fail in life until they stop putting in effort or give up.
Discuss the importance of demonstrating resilience in school and in life ...
Resilience allows people to overcome adversity and difficult times.
What emotions do you experience when you display resilience?
Pride, joy, determination, motivation, happiness
Share the relationship that exists between resilience and overcoming bullying/school violence ...
The more resilient a person is, the more able they are to overcome difficult times and move forward in a positive direction/not allow the difficult situation to define them.

Evidence-Based Practice: Stop That Negative Thought
- Students will record five thoughts that they have/negative self-talk statements that impede their growth.
- Students will then engage in thought stopping and as soon as they have that thought, practice stopping the thought/negative self-talk and replace it with a positive and motivating statement.
- Engaging in thought-stopping and positive self-talk can help to reframe negativity, motivate, and inspire students to persevere and overcome challenges.

Creative Activity: iWarrior
- Students will draw a caricature of themselves as a warrior.
- Students will use words, quotes, images, colors that depict bravery, strength, and courage.
- Next to their warrior image, students will record the following:
  - A time in my life when I faced adversity ...
  - What I learned about myself as a result of going through this challenging situation ...
  - Characteristics I possess that enable me to be resilient
  - Challenges I will still have to face ...

- Steps that I can take to overcome these challenges, as there is only one direction: moving forward

Discussion Questions:
In what ways does resilience help us to create a safer and healthier school climate?
What is the importance of working to overcome adversity and not allowing challenges to dictate who we become?
In what ways did this activity enable you to enhance your resilience?
How does resilience help us to work toward self-actualization; reaching our fullest potential?
Discuss how demonstrating resilience enables us to feel a sense of empowerment …

Feedback:
Counselors can either ask for verbal or written feedback in order to assess the impact of the session on student outcomes:

On a scale from one to five (1 being low and 5 being high) rate the following:
This session helped to raise my awareness of resilience.
This session helped me to recognize the impact that resilience has on my self-esteem and reaching my fullest potential.
This session helped me to recognize steps that I can take in order to amplify my resilience.
This session enabled me to recognize the significance of demonstrating resilience.

Elementary/Primary Activities to Become My Best SELf

Lesson Plan 1: Accountability

Lesson Plan Objective: To help students understand the definition of accountability, the importance of being accountable, and the ways to demonstrate accountability.

Materials: Markers, Paper, and Jello

Group Questions:

1. Ask students what does the word accountability means?
   Being in control, taking ownership, being responsible, not blaming others, agreeing to do something and doing it, acting in a trustworthy way ☺
2. Ask students what is the importance of accountability?
   Taking ownership for one's actions and behaving in a way that develops trust with others
3. What are some ways to demonstrate accountability?

Admitting to mistakes, apologizing for our mistakes, and following through on assigned tasks or commitments that we make.

Activity 1: Read Yertle the Turtle

Process:
Did Yertle demonstrate responsibility?
What could Yertle have done to be more responsible?
https://www.youtube.com/watch?v=b0NHrFNZWh0
Students and stakeholders will sing along to the Five Little Monkeys song
Process:
Were the monkeys being accountable/responsible?
What could the monkeys have done to be more responsible/accountable?
Activity 2: J-E-L-L-O Challenge ☺

* Stakeholders will assist students in making Jello.
* Each student will be responsible for a different task.
* Stakeholders will break up students into small groups.
* Stakeholders will give each student a direction/responsibility (all students must wash hands before making Jello).
* One student will get the bowl, one student will get the spoon, one student will get the ingredients.
* Students will listen to the stakeholders' instructions and be responsible for their roles. Upon completion, students will enjoy Jello ☺.

Follow-Up Questions:
What does it mean to be accountable?
What is the importance of being accountable/responsible?
What are some ways we can demonstrate accountability/show that we are responsible?
Group Feedback:
I enjoyed today's activity? ☺ or ☹
This activity helped me to understand the definition of accountability. ☺ or ☹
This activity helped me to understand the importance of accountability. ☺ or ☹

Lesson Plan 2: Emotion Identification

Lesson Plan Objective: To help students understand the definition of emotion identification, importance of being able to identify emotions, as well as strategies to use to identify emotions
Materials: Markers, Paper, Tape, and Feeling Cards

Group Questions:

1   Ask students what do emotions mean?
     Feelings we experience when something happens.
2   What are some types of emotions we can feel?
     Happy, sad, frustrated, angry, excited, surprised, embarrassed, afraid, anxious.
3   Ask students what is the importance of being able to identify an emotion or know how we feel?
     It helps us to talk about our feelings and express them rather than keep them bottled up inside.
4   Who can we talk to if we are feeling sad?
     Parents, family members, friends, teachers, coaches
5   What are some healthy ways we can show our emotions?

Talking, sharing, drawing, painting, playing

Activity 1:
Students will watch Emotion Identification Video in large group
https://www.youtube.com/watch?v=nTII0cyUbQo
Activity 2: Feelings Hop

* Tape feeling mats using emojis to the floor with tape (find emojis for anger, excitement, happiness, sadness, fear, embarrassment).
* For younger kids, only tape a few feelings to the ground in order to not overwhelm them.
* Stakeholders will call out a feeling and the students will hop and point to the feeling you state.
* Students must say how their body feels when they experience the emotion.
* Students will be asked to describe a time when they felt the emotion and stakeholders can give an example of how they felt when they experienced that emotion.

Activity 3: I Got This Feeling Inside My Heart <3 Activity
    Stakeholders will help students draw a large heart on a piece of construction paper and assist students in coloring in the heart with different colors that represent various emotions.

   Purple = Happy
   Blue = Sad
   Yellow = Worried
   Black=Scared
   Green = Mad
   Red = Frustrated
   Pink = Loved

Upon completion, stakeholders will process with students' reasons as to why their heart is filled with chosen emotion.

Activity 3: Feelings Wheel

Stakeholders will help students draw a Feeling Wheel by drawing a large circle and separating the circle into **six** equal sections. Each section of the Feelings Wheel will have its own emotion. Stakeholders will label each section within the Feelings Wheel: **Angry, Happy, Sad, Confused, Excited, and Proud.** Stakeholders will assist students with recording or drawing a picture illustrating a time when they experienced each of these emotions.

Follow-Up Questions:

What does it mean to identify our emotions?
What are some reasons why it is important to be able to identify emotions?
Who can we talk to when we are feeling sad or mad?
What are some healthy ways we can show our emotions?

Group Feedback:

I enjoyed today's activity? ☺ or ☹
This activity helped me to understand the definition of emotion identification. ☺ or ☹
This activity helped me to understand the importance of emotion identification. ☺ or ☹

Lesson Plan 3: Emotion Regulation

Lesson Plan Objective: To help students understand the definition of emotion regulation, the importance of emotion regulation, and ways to engage in emotion regulation.

Materials: Markers, Paper, Play Doh
Group Questions:

1   Ask students what does the word emotion regulation means?
    Being in control, being mindful, thinking before acting ☺
2   Ask students what is the importance of emotion regulation?
    To be in control, to focus, to pay attention, to not be disruptive, to stay on task, to be aware of consequences of behaviors/choices.
3   What are some ways to regulate our emotions?

Think before acting, count to five, keep post-its on the desk to remind us, logical consequences (tell me what will happen if you do this and tell me what will happen if you do not do this), mindfulness, meditate, and deep breathing.

Activity 1:

Sit in a circle and sing the Self-Control Song https://www.youtube.com/watch?v=pd7_GpERNOM and ask students what they liked about the song and how they can apply what they learned in the song to their own behavior.

Activity 2:
Stakeholders will review zones of regulation with students and review various colors associated with emotions

> **Blue:** Tired/Sad/Sick/Depressed
> **Green:** Happy/Thankful/Proud/Positive/Ready to Learn
> **Yellow:** Excited/Annoyed/Worried/Embarrassed/Confused
> **Red**: Upset/Angry/Aggressive/Loss of Control

Activity 3: Students will listen to a guided meditation addressing relaxation and self-control **(play 6 minutes of meditation)** https://www.youtube.com/watch?v=DWOHcGF1Tmc&t=82s
Upon completion process:
How did this meditation help you to feel in control?
What did you like most about this activity?
Discuss what was helpful about this activity …

Activity 4:
Students will work in small groups or dyads. Each small group of students will receive different colors of Play-Doh.

> **Red:** Frustrated
> **Yellow:** Worried
> **Blue:** Sad
> **Green:** Mad
> **Purple:** Happy

Stakeholders will work with students and help them to identify emotions/feelings associated with each color. Each small group of students will identify and mold emotions associated with each of the Play-Doh colors.

Follow-Up Questions:
What does it mean to regulate/be in control of our emotions?
What is the importance of emotion regulation?
What are some ways we can regulate our emotions?

Group Feedback:
I enjoyed today's activity? ☺ or ☹
This activity helped me to understand the definition of emotion regulation. ☺ or ☹
This activity helped me to understand the importance of emotion regulation. ☺ or ☹

Lesson Plan 4: Mindfulness

Lesson Plan Objective: To help students understand the definition of mindfulness, as well as the importance of staying present in order to demonstrate self-control and reduce impulsivity

Materials: Markers, Paper, Glue, Glitter, Computer, Jar/Water Bottle

Group Questions:

1   Ask students what does the word mindfulness means?
    Mindfulness entails being in the present, living in the immediate here and now, rather than focusing on the past or future. Focusing one's awareness on the present moment and noticing emotions and sensations without judgment.
2   Ask students what is the importance of mindfulness?
    It allows us to experience greater self-control, deeper focus, reduced stress, increased coping, increased control over anger, reduced hyperactivity, and a greater appreciation of the present.
3   What are some ways to engage in mindfulness?

Meditation, deep breathing, walking, cooking, chasing bubbles, drawing, storytelling, taking 5-minute breaks to notice sensations in the body, yoga.

Activity 1: Meditation

Students will listen to either:
The Dragon Story Time Meditation for Kids https://www.youtube.com/results?search_query=dragon+story+time+meditation
Mindfulness Meditation for Kids and complete deep breathing and mindfulness activities https://www.youtube.com/watch?v=Bk_qU7l-fcU
Your Magical Island Meditation https://www.youtube.com/watch?v=aNTXpJV8aUg
Rainbow Breath https://www.youtube.com/watch?v=O29e4rRMrV4&t=5s

Upon completion process:
How did this activity help you to feel centered?
What did you enjoy most about this activity?
Discuss how you can use mindfulness to feel present and focused …

Activity 2: Glitter Jar
Stakeholders will work with students in small groups to create glitter jars. When kids are sad, angry, or stressed, it is challenging for them to make healthy choices. Mindfulness helps to increase wellness and self-control. Kids can watch the glitter swirl to the bottom of the jar which provides

them time to calm down, regain control, and refocus their attention in a healthy manner. Each small group of students will receive a mini water bottle. Mini water bottles and glitter is needed for this activity

- Open caps on mini water bottles.
- Assist students in pouring glitter into the water bottle.
- Have the students shake the mini water bottle well to distribute glitter evenly.
- Students are encouraged to watch the glitter swirl and breathe deeply as they watch the glitter swirl to the bottom of the water bottle.
- Ask students to be mindful of the calming feeling in their body as they breathe.
- Encourage students to clear their unsettling thoughts and experience calmness as the glitter swirls to the bottom.
- The shaking glitter represents feeling unsettled, whereas the glitter that has settled represents calmness.

Follow-Up Questions:
What does it mean to be mindful?
What is the importance of using mindfulness when we feel ourselves losing control?
What are some ways we can use mindfulness at school and at home?

Group Feedback:
I enjoyed today's activity? ☺ or ☹
This activity helped me to understand the definition of mindfulness. ☺ or ☹
This activity helped me to understand the importance of mindfulness and feel a sense of calmness. ☺ or ☹

Lesson Plan 5: Coping Skills

Lesson Plan Objective: To help students understand the definition of coping skills, as well as the importance of coping skills when dealing with uncomfortable feelings including anger, sadness, frustration, or stress

Materials: Markers, Paper, Brown Paper Bag, and Paper Strips
Group Questions:

1 Ask students what does coping skills mean?
   Skills that we possess that enable us to deal with stressful situations.
2 Ask students what is the importance of possessing coping skills?
   We are able to deal with and overcome situations that elicit uncomfortable feelings in a healthy, proactive, and efficient way.
3 What are some examples of coping skills?

Deep breathing, writing, drawing, journaling, tapping, listening to music, artwork, exercise, communication.

Activity 1:
Stakeholders can complete the Positive Self-Talk Armor Activity using the template below

Positive Self-Talk Armor Template

Things I Can Say To Myself That Protect Myself From Negativity

1
2
3
4
5

Emotions I Feel When I Wear My Protective Armor

1
2
3

Ways I Can Protect Myself In The Future From Negative Statements

1
2
3

Activity 2: Anger Bag
Stakeholders will help students create Anger Bags, which are excellent tools that enable students to record, release, purge, and separate the anger they are experiencing from themselves and externalize rather than internalize this uncomfortable feeling.

- Decorate a brown paper bag with images/colors/words that represent anger.
- Students name their "anger."
- Students record their anger triggers on strips of white paper.
- Students process anger triggers out loud.
- Students crumple up strips of paper and throw into a bag, as a way to purge themselves of the anger they are experiencing.

Follow-Up Questions:
In what ways did this activity help you to improve your coping skills?

Discuss additional coping skills you can use when feeling angry, sad, hurt, or frustrated …

What is the importance of possessing effective coping skills?

Group Feedback:

I enjoyed today's activity? ☺ or ☹

This activity helped me to understand the definition of coping skills. ☺ or ☹

This activity helped me to understand the importance of possessing effective coping skills when experiencing an uncomfortable feeling. ☺ or ☹

Lesson Plan 6: Resilience

Lesson Plan Objective: To help students understand the definition of resilience, as well as the importance of demonstrating resilience when facing adversity. We must persevere and not allow challenges to dictate who we become.

Materials: Markers, Paper, Art Supplies

Group Questions:

1   Ask students what does resilience means?
     Resilience means that we bounce back and do not allow hardships and adversity to define us and overpower us. We never fail in life until we stop trying.
2   Ask students what is the importance of demonstrating resilience?
     Resilience enables us to overcome any obstacles and work towards achieving our dreams and goals despite challenges that we may face along the way.
3   Who is your superhero and how has this person demonstrated resilience?
4   What are some qualities that resilient people possess?

Strength, righteousness, integrity, courage, bravery, fortitude, tenacity perseverance, and goal-oriented.

Activity 1: Beauty Is in the Eyes of the Beholder

Stakeholders can read the book, "*The Ugly Duckling*" to the class https://www.amazon.com/Ugly-Duckling-Caldecott-Honor-Book/dp/068815932X

Upon completion, ask students the following:

In what ways did the ugly duckling demonstrate resilience?

What were some challenges the ugly duckling faced?

What was the moral of this story?

Activity 2· I Think Therefore I am a Superhero

Stakeholders will work with students and assist students in drawing themselves as superheroes. Use the template below:

Draw yourself as a superhero on a separate piece of paper

Superhero
Name: _____

Superhero Power:
Superhero Mantra:

_____

_____

Qualities that you possess that make you resilient

1
2
3

One way in which you have demonstrated resilience (overcame a challenge)
What did you learn about yourself as a result of the experience?
If you could be anything in life, what would you be?

_____

_____

_____

If you could do one thing to make the world a better place, what would you do?

Follow-Up Questions:

In what ways did this activity help you to understand the importance of demonstrating resilience?

Discuss the importance of demonstrating resilience when faced with challenges …

Indicate the importance of persevering in school and in life …

Group Feedback:

I enjoyed today's activity? ☺ or ☹

This activity helped me to understand the definition of resilience. ☺ or ☹

This activity helped me to understand the importance of demonstrating resilience and persevering so I can reach my fullest potential. ☺ or ☹

References

DeBerard, M. S., Speilmans, G. I., & Julka, D. L. (2004). Predictors of academic achievement and retention among college freshmen: A longitudinal study. *College Student Journal, 38*(1), 66–80.

Gullone, E., Hughes, E. K., King, N. J., & Tonge, B. (2010). The normative development of emotion regulation strategy use in children and adolescents: A 2-year follow-up study. *Journal of Child Psychology and Psychiatry, 51*, 567–574.

Weissberg, R. (2016). *Why social and emotional learning is essential for students.* Retrieved from https://www.edutopia.org/blog/why-sel-essential-for-students-weissberg-durlak-domitrovich-gullotta.

17 Social Awareness

Taking the perspective of and empathizing with others who may differ from you, as well as appreciating others' and their differences. This entails the ability to understand, empathize, and feel compassion from those who have different backgrounds and or ideologies (Weissberg, 2016). One fundamental aspect of social awareness of to be able to respect and celebrate others' perspectives in various social interactions and settings, which promotes pro-social behavior (Decety, 2009). Further, social awareness allows people to recognize situations in which social support is vital in regard to conflict resolution and problem-solving. For instance, having peer support and having study groups may help students understand concepts from other perspectives, learn material, and promote greater academic success.

Secondary Activities

Lesson Plan 1: Diversity

Directions: This activity can be facilitated in a classroom, small group, or individual counseling setting. First, the definition of diversity will be addressed. Students will then process open-ended questions, complete the evidence-based practice activity, the creative activity, follow-up discussion questions in order to review material learned, as well as feedback questions to assess the impact of the session on student learning outcomes.

Definition of Diversity: Practice of including or involving people from a range of different backgrounds. Range of human differences regarding race, ethnicity, religious beliefs, ideologies, sexual orientation, and abilities.

Open-Ended Questions:
When you think of the word "diversity, "what adjectives come to mind?
Differences, similarities, celebration, various perspectives
What is the importance of having diversity in the classroom, school, society at large?
Diversity allows us to learn from one another, break down barriers, and have a more inclusive and responsive climate.

DOI: 10.4324/9781003262183-17

Discuss the importance for stakeholders to experience inclusion, belonging, and acceptance ....
Belonging allows people to feel understood, validated, a sense of acceptance, and importance.
Share things that we can do in school to celebrate diversity ...
Have discussions about culture, celebrate different cultures each month, invite families in to discuss values and beliefs, create a climate that is welcoming and accepting to all.

Evidence-Based Activity: Reframe to End Shame

- Students will fold a piece of paper in half.
- Students will record five stereotypes regarding their culture of origin on one side of the paper.
- On the other side of the paper, students will challenge stereotypes and provide a positive reframe for each stereotype listed.

Creative Activity 1: Diversity Self-Assessment
Students will record responses to the following individually. Upon completion debrief in a group:

- Human difference topics that I need to become more informed about include ...
- Hesitations or fears I have of interacting with others who are different from me include ...
- Qualities I possess that enable me to be culturally responsive include ...
- It is important to be able to accept and work with all different types of people because ...
- Steps that I can take to enhance my cultural responsiveness/sensitivity include ...

Creative Activity 2: Restorative Justice Circle on Diversity
Have students sit in a circular formation, as this helps to promote engagement

- Have students record one issue that impacts them personally (academically/socially/emotionally) regarding diversity.
- Have students read aloud their responses.
- In a circle, have an open dialogue about each of these topics in order to foster self-disclosure, learning, and awareness.

We have to have conversations/open dialogue and use our platform to promote systemic change. Doing so helps to foster inclusion, validation, and acceptance of all.

Creative Activity 3: Standing Up To ISMs

- Discuss each ISM including racism, ageism, socialism, classism, anti-semitism, ableism, and heterosexism.
- Call out each ISM and have students stand up by their desks if they have experienced an ISM directly or if they know someone who has experienced an ISM.
- Ask students to share their experience in order to process, raise awareness, encourage open dialogue, understanding, and create a more accepting and culturally responsive climate.

Discussion Questions

In what ways is recognizing diversity essential?

What are steps that we can take to create a more culturally responsive climate at school based on conversations today?

In what ways did these activities help to raise your awareness about the importance of diversity and cultural responsiveness?

Share the significance of recognizing bias/stereotypes in order to become more culturally responsive...

Discuss the importance of talking about diversity in order to have a safer and more inclusive school and workforce...

Feedback:

Counselors can either ask for verbal or written feedback in order to assess the impact of the session on student outcomes:

On a scale from one to five (1 being low and 5 being high) rate the following:

- This session helped to raise my awareness about diversity.
- This session helped me to recognize the impact that diversity has on my academic performance, social skills, and behaviors.
- This session helped me to recognize the skills I need to build in order to improve my cultural responsiveness.
- This session provided me with tools I can use to enhance my cultural responsiveness.
- This session helped me to become more cognizant of the importance of cultural humility and sensitivity in order to have a safer and more secure school climate, as well as a collaborative workforce.

Elementary/Primary Activities to Become My Best SELf

Lesson Plan 1: Kindness

Lesson Plan Topic: Kindness

Lesson Plan Objective: To help students understand the definition of kindness, qualities of a kind person, as well as the importance of demonstrating kindness.

Materials: Markers, Paper

Group Questions:

1 **Ask students what does the word kindness means?**
   Use kind words, being nice, treating people the way we want to be treated.
2 **Ask students what are some words that remind you of showing kindness/caring?**
   Empathy, friendship, respect, equality, love, understanding, patience
3 **How would you describe a kind/caring person?**
   Someone who is generous, thoughtful, selfless, a good friend, empathic, a good listener, and nice to everyone.
4 **What is the importance of being kind/caring inside and out of the classroom?**

Helps us to feel welcome, included, form and maintain friendships, act as role models, reduce bullying, treat others the way we want to be treated.

Activity 1: Kindness Chain
Discuss how a chain of kindness encourages others to be kind. When one person does something that is kind, others can model that behavior. Using different colored construction paper, stakeholders can assist students in forming chains of kindness and writing down ways they can demonstrate caring and kindness to others. Upon completion, hang the kindness chain in the classroom or your office.

Activity 2: Bee Kind

- Stakeholders will trace and cut out a large bumblebee and decorate the bee with googly eyes and antennas prior to class/group.
- On the bumblebee, students will each write down ways that they can demonstrate kindness in class, during lunch, at recess, on the bus, and at home.
- The bumblebee creation will be hung up in the classroom or office.

Follow-Up Questions:
What does it mean to be kind?
What types of words remind you of kindness/caring?
In what ways is it important to be kind?

Group Feedback:
I enjoyed today's activity? ☺ or ☹
This activity helped me to understand the definition of kindness/caring. ☺ or ☹
This activity helped me to understand the importance of showing kindness/caring. ☺ or ☹

Lesson Plan 2: Respect

Lesson Plan Objective: To help students understand the definition of respect, the qualities of a respectful person, as well as the importance of demonstrating respect.

Materials: Markers, Paper

Group Questions:

1   **Ask students what does the word respect means?**
     Value and appreciate others, admire others, follow rules.
2   **Ask students what are some words that remind you of showing respect?**
     Listening, empathy, kindness, equality, compassion, understanding.
3   **How would you describe a respectful person?**
     Someone who treats others the way they want to be treated, open-minded, flexible, understanding, and accepting.
4   **What is the importance of being respectful inside and out of the classroom?**
     Respect helps to foster friendships, connectivity, relationships, promotes collaboration, togetherness, cohesion, and peace.

Activity 1: RESPECT Adjectives
On the cutout letters RESPECT, stakeholders will help students think of words that represent each letter

Activity 2: R-E-S-P-E-C-T Activity
Stakeholders will read the following brief guided visualization activity and upon completion, students will respond to questions.

Students will verbally respond to the following:

*   What colors do you associate with respect?
*   How would this group/class/school be different if everyone showed respect to one another?
*   What emotions do you experience when you give and show respect?
*   Each student will state one way they can demonstrate greater respect.
*   Sit on the floor in a crisscross applesauce position.
*   Close your eyes and take three deep breaths in.
*   I want you to imagine what this group, class, and school would look like if everyone was respectful to one another.
*   Imagine the colors you see when you think of respect.
*   Think about the emotions you would feel if everyone was respectful toward one another.
*   Slowly open your eyes and be present.

Follow-Up Questions:
What does it mean to be respectful?

What types of words remind you of respect?
In what ways is it important to be respectful?

Small-Group Feedback:
I enjoyed today's activity? ☺ or ☹
This activity helped me to understand the definition of respect. ☺ or ☹
This activity helped me to understand the importance of showing respect.
☺ or ☹

Lesson Plan 3: Listening

Lesson Plan Objective: To help students understand the definition of listening, the importance of communication and listening, and the ways to improve listening.

Materials: Markers, Paper, Streganonna Book, Construction Paper

Large Group Questions:

1 **Ask students what does the word listening mean?**
   To understand and attentively hear what another is saying ☺
2 **Ask students what is the importance of listening?**
   We understand one another, we hear other people's ideas, we feel understood, and we are able to express ourselves
3 **What is the importance of listening inside and out of class?** Learning, directions, we know what to do, we hear one another, we show respect

Activity 1: Pasta Pasta Pasta
Read the book, *Strega Nona*, to the class
https://www.amazon.com/Strega-Nona-Tomie-dePaola/dp/0671666061/
ref=sr_1_1?crid=V97Q3KM6S8PB&dchild=1&keywords=strega+nona
+books&qid=1589647722&sprefix=strega%2Caps%2C238&sr=8-1

Process:
Did Big Anthony listen to *Strega Nona*?
What happened as a result of his not listening?
Discuss what Anthony could have done differently ...

Activity 2: Listen to the Beat Activity
Using different items and materials, stakeholders will ask students to identify what sounds they heard **(keys, beads, chimes, pencil dropping, whistle).** Students will be turned around and asked to close their eyes so they cannot see the object being used—they must use their listening skills.

Process:
In what ways did this activity help to improve your listening skills?

Activity 3: Simon Says

Briefly play Simon Says: Stakeholders will work with a group of students and play Simon Says. Stakeholders will say the commands including:

- Laugh
- Jump
- Point out of the window
- Look down/up
- Make a funny face
- Stand on one foot
- Act like a robot, dance
- Write in the air
- Sing
- Moo like a cow
- Shake
- Hop like a bunny
- Sit down
- Stand up
- Wave
- Show your muscles
- Stand behind a chair

Follow-Up Questions:
How did these activities enable you to improve your listening skills?
What is the importance of listening?
What are some things we can do to become better listeners?

Group Feedback:
I enjoyed today's activity? ☺ or ☹
This activity helped me to understand the definition of listening. ☺ or ☹
This activity helped me to understand the importance of listening. ☺ or ☹

Lesson Plan 4: Empathy

Lesson Plan Objective: To help students understand the definition of empathy, the importance of empathy, and the ways to show empathy.

Materials: Markers, Paper, Computer, and Construction Paper

Group Questions:

1 **Ask students what does the word empathy means?**
   Compassionate, feeling what someone else is feeling, relating to their feelings. ☺
2 **Ask students what is the importance of empathy?**
   People feel understood, comforted, accepted, and supported.

3   **What are some ways to show empathy?**

Imagine how you would feel if you were going through the same situation, put yourself in that person's shoes; show kindness, listen, give hugs, praise.

Activity 1: Empathy Clip
Students will watch a clip addressing empathy
https://www.youtube.com/watch?v=ka5pSiyJ5ok
and discuss the importance of empathy and what they learned from watching the clip.

•   Ask students what we can do when our friends are feeling sad?
•   What does it mean to show empathy?
•   In what ways is empathy different from sympathy?

Activity 2: My Rainbow and I Activity
Stakeholders will assist students in making their My Rainbow and I Activity. Stakeholders will cut out clouds and colored strips of paper prior to the class/group. Each student will make a name rainbow using pre-cut clouds and colored strips of paper. On the cloud, students will write their name and on the strips of colored paper, students will record adjectives that represent each letter of their name, as well as how they are empathic. Once completed, each student in the class/group will state one way in which they can demonstrate greater empathy.

Empathy Certificate: Each student will receive a printed empathy certificate found below

Empathy Certificate

Name of Student:

Date:

Ways Student Displays Empathy:

Follow-Up Questions:
What does empathy mean?
What is the importance of showing empathy?
What are some ways we can show empathy?

Group Feedback:
I enjoyed today's activity? ☺ or ☹
This activity helped me to understand the definition of empathy. ☺ or ☹
This activity helped me to understand the importance of empathy. ☺ or ☹

Lesson Plan 5: Impact of Behaviors on Others/Bullying

Lesson Plan Topic: Impact of Behaviors on Others/Bullying

Lesson Plan Objective: To help students understand the impact of one's own behavior on others, teach students the definition of bullying, qualities of a bully, reasons why kids bully, consequences of bullying, as well as the importance of standing up to a bully. ☺

Materials: Markers, Paper, Llama Llama and the Bully Goat Book, Poster Board

Group Questions:

1 **Discuss the importance of being aware of how one's behavior impacts others ...**
   We must be aware of how our behavior impacts others in order to have a safe and nurturing class and treat our peers the way we want to be treated.
2 **Ask students what does the word bully means?**
   When someone repeatedly and intentionally hurts others through words or action.
3 **Ask students what are some qualities of a bully?**
   Mean, controlling, powerful, scary, hurtful, embarrassing
4 **How do kids feel if they are bullied?**
   Sad, upset, angry, powerless, hurt, ashamed
5 **Why do kids bully other kids?**
   They may want attention, want to be feared, want to control others, feel bad about themselves, may be jealous, or angry.
6 **Indicate some consequences of bullying ...**
   Sadness, anger, frustration, hopelessness, depression, anxiety, isolation, thoughts of self-harm.
7 **What is the importance of standing up to a bully?** So our friends feel safe, create a kinder class, assert ourselves (confidently), put a stop to mean/cruel behavior.

Activity 1: Read book '*Llama Llama and the Bully Goat*'
Ask students:

1 How did llama feel when he was bullied?
2 What happened when the goat bullied the other kids?
3 What did you learn about bullying after hearing the story?
4 What is the importance of treating others the way you want to be treated?

Activity 2: Apologizing
Stakeholders will teach students about the importance of apologizing if they have been mean to someone. Have each student go around the circle

and talk about a time they did not treat someone kindly. Using the empty chair technique, have each student practice apologizing. In a clear voice, have each student practice saying "I am sorry I _____." Stakeholders will act as the person in the empty chair and after each student apologizes stakeholders will state, "I forgive you. Thank you for being so brave."

Activity 3: Friendly Frank Face Poster

- Stakeholders will cut out a large image of a face using poster paper.
- Stakeholders will brainstorm with students' qualities that good friends possess, as well as ways in which they can be good friends and record these ideas on Friendly Frank's Face.
- The poster will be hung up in the classroom/office to remind them of the importance of creating a bully-free classroom zone and being a good friend. ☺

Follow-Up Questions

What does it mean to be a bully?
What are some reasons kids bully other kids?
In what ways is it important to stand up to bullies?

Small-Group Feedback:

I enjoyed today's activity? ☺ or ☹
This activity helped me to understand the importance of being aware of the impact of my actions on others. ☺ or ☹
This activity helped me to understand the importance of being a good friend, being socially aware, and creating a bully-free class. ☺ or ☹

Lesson Plan 6: Citizenship

Lesson Plan Objective: To help students understand the definition of citizenship, qualities of a helpful person, as well as the importance of demonstrating citizenship.

Materials: Markers, Paper, Crown Template, Popsicle Sticks, Glue

Group Questions:

1 **Ask students what does the word citizenship mean?**
   Cooperation, helper, involvement, following rules
2 **Ask students what are some words that remind you of showing good citizenship?**
   Kindness, leader, helper, understanding, and a positive role model
3 **How would you describe a person who shows good citizenship?**
   Effective decision-maker, mensch, good doer, role model, and leader

4   **What is the importance of being helpful/cooperative inside and out of the classroom?**

Sets a positive example for others, demonstrates caring and respect, fosters productivity, promotes listening, and encourages collaboration.

Activity 1: Helpers are Heroes

As a class, talk about how sometimes we *help* and sometimes we *need help*. People who help are not only good citizens but also heroes.

- Students will work in small groups.
- Stakeholders will set out various cardboard boxes in which students can decorate and draw pictures of how they may need help.
- Upon completion, in a large circle, stakeholders will discuss the pictures that students drew and process with the students' ways in which they can help one another overcome the problem illustrated.

Activity 2: Crown Me for My Citizenship

- Students will draw and cut out a crown image using construction paper.
- Glue a popsicle stick behind the crown.
- On the crown, students will record one quality they possess that makes them an impactful citizen in order to showcase their citizenship regally.
- Upon completion, students will share their masterpieces with one another.

Follow-Up Questions:
What does it mean to be a good citizen?
What types of words remind you of citizenship?
In what ways is it important to be a good citizen?

Group Feedback:
I enjoyed today's activity? ☺ or ☹
This activity helped me to understand the definition of citizenship. ☺ or ☹
This activity helped me to understand the importance of showing citizenship. ☺ or ☹

References

Decety, J. (2009). *The social neuroscience of empathy*. Cambridge, MA: MIT Press.
Weissberg, R. (2016). *Why social and emotional learning is essential for students.* Retrieved from https://www.edutopia.org/blog/why-sel-essential-for-students-weissberg-durlak-domitrovich-gullotta

18 Relationship Skills

Includes maintaining healthy and cooperative relationships, fostering connectivity, and increasing social support (Mattanah, Ayers, Brand, Brooks, Quimby, McNary, 2010), preventing interpersonal conflict, and working through conflict peacefully when needed. Relationship skills help students build and maintain healthy relationships, demonstrate optimism, act in accordance with social norms, as well as communicate, actively listen, cooperate, negotiate conflict, and seek assistance when needed (Weissberg, 2016). Additionally, relationship skills help students to work better collaboratively and with those from diverse backgrounds. Relationship skills also help students to build support networks, as well as encourages students to seek out help when needed in order to obtain academic, personal, social, and vocational guidance.

Secondary Activities

Lesson Plan 1: Conflict Resolution

Directions: This activity can be facilitated in a classroom, small group, or individual counseling setting. First, the definition of conflict resolution will be addressed. Students will then process open-ended questions, complete the evidence-based practice activity, the creative activity, follow-up discussion questions in order to review material learned, as well as feedback questions to assess the impact of the session on student learning outcomes.

Definition of Conflict Resolution: Process that people go through to peacefully resolve a struggle or problem.

Open-Ended Questions
What comes to mind when you hear about conflict resolution?
Problem solving, unity, getting along.
In what ways is it important to resolve conflicts peacefully?
Talking, actively listening, showing respect, validating all perspectives.
Discuss the role that active listening plays in problem-solving…
Active listening promotes understanding, validation, and empowerment.

DOI: 10.4324/9781003262183-18

Share the qualities you possess that help you to be an effective problem solver ...
Compassionate, leadership skills, patience, strong nonverbal communication skills.

What are some consequences faced if people lack effective conflict resolution skills?
Argue, lack of productivity, lack of efficiency

Evidence-Based Practice 1: Conflict Resolution Questionnaire in order to obtain a baseline measure of the degree to which students possess conflict resolution skills.
https://studentlifeguru.files.wordpress.com/2013/08/conflict-question naire.pdf

Evidence-Based Practice 2: Scaling Questions
On a scale from one to five (1 being low and 5 being high) rate the following:

- Rate the degree to which you feel equipped to solve problems
- Rate the degree to which you have been able to solve problems in the past peacefully
- Rate your ability to effectively listen
- Rate your ability to engage in perspective sharing
- Rate your ability to take ownership of the role that you played in the conflict

Creative Activity 1: Problem Solved Scenarios

- The counselor will write down various scenarios on strips of paper.
- The counselor will put strips of paper containing scenarios in a bowl.
- Students will randomly choose a scenario, read the scenario out loud, and in a group collaboratively process ways to resolve the given conflict peacefully.

Potential Scenario Topics:

- A student is talking behind another student's back. Both the students are friends.
- A student feels left out from his/her group of friends.
- A student's friend starts dating the person the student likes and his/her friend knew this prior to dating them.
- A student's friend is engaging in attention-seeking behavior on social media.
- A student is being taunted in class.

Creative Activity 2: Master Problem Solver
Students will briefly record responses to the following:

- The conflict you recently faced.

- Emotions you experienced during the conflict.
- Your role in the conflict.
- Steps you took to resolve the conflict.

Discussion Questions:
In what ways is enhancing conflict resolution skills vital?
How did these activities help you to improve your conflict resolution skills?
What needs to happen in order to peacefully resolve conflict?
Share what steps you can take in the future to further improve your conflict resolution skills...

Feedback:
Counselors can either ask for verbal or written feedback in order to assess the impact of the session on student outcomes:
On a scale from one to five (1 being low and 5 being high) rate the following:

- This session helped to raise my awareness about conflict resolution.
- This session helped me to recognize the impact that conflict resolution has on my emotions and social skills.
- This session helped me to recognize the skills I need to build in order to improve my conflict resolution abilities.
- This session provided me with tools I can use to enhance my conflict resolution skills.
- This session helped me to feel more accomplished and proud of my ability to resolve conflicts peacefully.

Bullying Intervention

Directions: This intervention is six weeks in length and can be implemented in a classroom, small group, or individual setting. Each session within the intervention will be composed of evidence-based practice activity, a creative activity, and follow-up discussion questions in order to ensure rigor and critical thinking. At the end of the 6-week intervention, feedback questions will be asked in order to assess the efficacy of the intervention on student learning outcomes.

Session 1: Overview of Bullying

Goals and Expectations of Group: For each student to share, learn, and understand the impact of bullying on social/emotional, psychological, behavioral, and academic performance. Overarching goal for students is to learn skills necessary to overcome being a victim of bullying.

Rules of Group: Be respectful, attendance, active listening, and participation

Bullying Definition: Unwanted and aggressive behavior that involves having a power imbalance. Behavior is repetitive and intentional. Bullying must consist of having an imbalance of power in regard to physical strength, embarrassing information being shared, or popularity/influence. Bullying is repetitive and happens more than once

Evidence-Based Practice: Students will complete the Personal Experiences Checklist in order to provide baseline feedback regarding the extent to which they are experiencing bullying https://www.mq.edu.au/__data/assets/pdf_file/0016/503512/PECK_Checklist_2015_copyright_V2.pdf

Creative Activity: In a round-robin circle, each student in the group will share the following:

- Share your experiences with bullying.
- Indicate the emotions you experience when being bullied.
- Discuss how bullying has impacted you personally, socially, academically.
- Indicate one coping strategy you currently use to help you overcome bullying.

Discussion Questions:

In what way did this group help you to understand the concept of bullying?

What is the importance of reporting being bullied?

How was this session awareness raising?

In what ways is it important to talk about our feelings; especially when experiencing bullying?

Session 2: Shame

Definition of Shame: A painful feeling of humiliation or distress caused by the consciousness of wrong or foolish behavior.

Evidence-Based Practice: Students can record five negative statements/criticisms that they say to themselves that evoke feelings of shame. Students can then work on providing positive reframes to each of these negative statements in order to challenge and modify negative thoughts **Example:** Negative Statement: "I am not worthy."

Positive Reframe: "I am deserving of happiness and choose to be happy every day."

Creative Activity:
- Students will draw what shame looks like to them.
- Students will use colors, shapes, images, and words that reflect shame.
- Students will process the types of emotions they experience when feeling shame.
- Students will share how they are currently coping.

- Upon completion, students will then process other coping techniques that can be used to process and release feelings of shame in a healthier way.

Discussion Questions:
In what ways did this session help you to challenge negative/unhealthy thoughts?
How is reframing an effective tool to use when experiencing negative thoughts?
What are some coping strategies you can use in the future in order to reduce feelings of shame?

Session 3: Fear

Define Fear: Unpleasant emotion caused by the belief that someone or something is dangerous or likely to cause pain.

Evidence-Based Practice: Students will briefly journal about a time in their lives they experienced fear when being bullied and record how that experience has impacted them. Upon completion, in a round-robin setting, students will process their experience, as well as what they have learned about themselves as a result of going through this experience (this is vital, as it allows students to recognize their strength and ability to survive and overcome adversity).

Creative Activity: Using black construction paper and whipped cream, students will illustrate what fear looks like to them. Once they complete their whipped cream image of fear, process the following:

- How does your body feel when you experience fear?
- What do you do when feeling fearful?
- Where is your safe place?
- Who is your safe person?

Let us process some healthy ways of coping with fear...

- Deep breathing
- Talking
- Writing
- Mindfulness
- Reframing

Discussion Questions:
In what ways did this session allow you to release some of the fear you have experienced?

What is the importance of identifying a secure place/person in your life? Indicate one coping strategy you can utilize in the future if you are experiencing fear…

Session 4: Assertiveness

Definition of Assertiveness: Quality of being self-assured and confident without being passive or aggressive.

Evidence-Based Practice: Students will complete the Rathus Scale to obtain a baseline measure of their level of assertiveness https://www.cengage.com/resource_uploads/downloads/0495092746_63633.pdf

Creative Activity: I Messages
Students will practice I Messages in order to enhance their assertiveness skills. Students will follow this template when practicing "I Messages": I feel _____ when you _____ please stop

Students will apply "I Messages" to the following situations:

*   The student finds out her friend is talking about her.
*   The student is being teased.
*   The student is being intentionally left out.
*   The student is being harassed on the bus.
*   The student is having rumors spread about him/her.

Discussion Questions:
What is the importance of demonstrating assertiveness?
In what ways can asserting yourself help you to feel more in control?
What are some steps that you can take in the future to be more assertive?

Session 5: Leadership

Define Leadership: The position of being a leader

Evidence-Based Practice: Miracle Question
In a round-robin circle, ask the following question to each student: If a miracle occurred and the bullying stopped, what in your life would be different regarding your leadership?

Creative Activity: Vision Plate
Students will create a vision plate using a white paper plate and Sharpie markers. On the plate students will do the following:

*   Identify five SMART goals that they would like to attain
*   Draw images of the SMART Goals students plan to work toward achieving

- The vision plate reflects the mantra seeing --> believing --> achieving, if we visualize our goals we are then more likely to take steps to achieve them.

Discussion Questions:

What is the importance of demonstrating leadership skills?

In what ways does setting goals help us to enhance our leadership skills?

How is creating a Vision Plate beneficial in motivating you to achieve your SMART Goals?

Session 6: Self-Love

Definition of Self-Love: Having high regard for oneself, one's well-being, and happiness. Self-love involves taking care of one's own needs in order to show oneself care and compassion.

Evidence-Based Practice: Positive Affirmations

All student participants will say **three** positive affirmations/comments that they love most about themselves. Students should be encouraged to say positive affirmations everyday in the morning in the mirror. Saying positive affirmations fosters a positive mindset, as well as feelings of empowerment.

Examples of Positive Affirmations: "I am loved" "I belong" "I am kind"

Creative Activity: Me, Myself, and I

- Students will write down their name.
- Next to each letter of their name, students will record a positive word/attribute that corresponds to the letter in their name.
- Students will also each process how they have grown as a result of being in the group, as well as state **one** positive statement/strength about the person sitting next to them.

Discussion Questions:

In what ways is it important to love yourself?

What is the significance of saying positive affirmations in order to boost self-love?

Discuss what you can do in the future to love yourself more?

Intervention Feedback Questions

On a scale from one to five (1 being low and 5 being high) rate the following:

- Rate the degree to which this group helped to raise your awareness about bullying and the consequences of bullying.
- Rate the degree to which this group helped you to process feelings of shame related to bullying.

- Rate the degree to which this group helped you to overcome feelings of fear related to bullying.
- Rate the degree to which this group helped you to enhance your assertiveness skills.
- Rate the degree to which this group helped you to enhance your leadership skills.
- Rate the degree to which this group helped you to enhance your self-love.

Additional Comments:

Elementary/Primary Activities to Become My Best SELf

Lesson Plan 1: Conflict Resolution

Lesson Plan Objective: To help students understand the definition of conflict resolution, qualities of a person who possesses problem-solving skills, as well as the importance of possessing conflict resolution skills.

Materials: Markers, Paper, Construction Paper, Googly Eyes, Glitter

Group Questions:

1 **Ask students what does the word conflict resolution means?**
   Problem-solving, win–win, getting to yes ☺
2 **Ask students what are some qualities that people with effective problem-solving skills possess?**
   Good listeners, fair, kind, open-minded, solution-focused, responsible
3 **What is the importance of possessing conflict resolution skills?**
   Ability to solve problems, to work well with others, to understand others' ideas, to be respectful, to achieve a win–win outcome.

Activity 1: I Came, I Saw, I Conquered Conflict Activity
Stakeholders will discuss the importance of staying calm, sharing how one feels, brainstorming solutions, and agreeing on a compromise when problem-solving effectively. Students will complete the activity using the template below:
   Record three things in your life that cause conflict between you and your peers:

1
2
3

Indicate five strategies you can use if someone is irritating you as a way to peacefully avoid conflict

1

2

3

4

5

Record **one** "**I Message**" you can use if someone is doing something that is upsetting to you. "I Messages" allow you to assert and express yourself in a confident way.

Example: I feel _____ when you _____ because_____. Please stop.
_____
_____

What emotions do you experience when you solve and conquer problems peacefully?
_____
_____

What can you do in the future to enhance your problem-solving skills like a conflicted warrior?
_____
_____

Activity 2: Glitter Problem Solver Poster

• Using glue, stakeholders can write the words "problem solver" in glue on black construction paper and cover the word with gold/silver glitter.
• Underneath the word, "Problem Solver," students will use white chalk to write down one adjective that they possess that makes them skillful problem solvers.

Follow-Up Questions:
What does conflict resolution mean?
What types of words remind you of conflict resolution?
In what ways is it important to be a problem solver?

Group Feedback:
I enjoyed today's activity? ☺ or ☹
This activity helped me to understand the definition of conflict resolution. ☺ or ☹
This activity helped me to understand the importance of possessing conflict resolution skills. ☺ or ☹

Lesson Plan 2: Communication

Lesson Plan Objective: To help students understand the definition of communication, as well as the importance of possessing strong communication skills.

Materials: Markers, Paper, and Index Cards

Group Questions:

1   **Ask students what does the word communication means?**
    To talk to, express oneself, listen, validate, understand, and interact with others who have similar and different perspectives/view points.
2   **Ask students what are some qualities that people with effective communication skills possess?**
    Good listeners, open-minded, respectful, patient, flexible, other-oriented, self-aware, and compassionate.
3   **What is the importance of possessing strong communication skills?**
    Communication allows us to express ourselves, collaborate, enables efficiency, understanding, leadership, and productivity.

Activity 1: It Is A Charade!

*   Stakeholders will develop topics that students can act out while playing Charades.
*   Charades will enable students to practice, utilize, and enhance their verbal and nonverbal communication skills (eye contact, posture, proximity, body language).
*   Sample topics can include book titles, movies, cartoon characters, songs, games, tasks, and their peers will need to attentively and critically determine the action being modeled.
*   Example: Sponge Bob Square Pants: Students can draw a square and point to a pair of pants.

Activity 2: 30 Seconds to Mars
Stakeholders will assist students in determining appropriate subjects to talk about addressing music, sports, celebrities, family, or stressors. Stakeholders will:

*   Choose one person in the group to start the conversation.
*   Students must make eye contact and be mindful of verbal/nonverbal communication.
*   If a student hesitates, repeats a word, or loses eye contact then another student in the group says "**error**" and that student takes over the conversation.

- Whoever is left talking at the end of 30 seconds wins the game. ☺

Activity 3: iCommunication
Students will complete the iCommunication Activity using the template below

1 On a scale from 1 to 5 (1 being lowest and 5 being highest), I rate my communication skills as a _____.

2 What qualities do you possess that make you an effective communicator?

_____

_____

3 How does it feel when you are talking and you feel as though you are not being heard?

_____

_____

4 If you could improve **one** communication skill, what would it be?

_____

_____

5 Indicate steps you can take to further improve your communication skills ...

a

b

c

6 In what ways will improving your communication skills help you to be more successful in school?

_____

_____

Follow-Up Questions:
In what ways is possessing communication skills important?
What steps can you take to improve your communication skills?
In what ways did this activity help you to be mindful of communication skills you excel in, as well as communication skills you can improve?

Group Feedback:
I enjoyed today's activity? ☺ or ☹
This activity helped me to understand the definition of communication. ☺ or ☹
This activity helped me to understand the importance of possessing strong communication skills. ☺ or ☹

Lesson Plan 3: Problem Solving

Lesson Plan Objective: To help students understand the definition of problem-solving, as well as the importance of possessing strong problem-solving skills.

Materials: Markers, Paper, Swedish Fish, Ruler, Plastic Cups, and Paper Clips

Group Questions:

1   **Ask students what does the word problem-solving means?**
    To work diligently toward solving a problem in a peaceful and cooperative manner.
2   **Ask students what are some qualities that people with effective problem solving possess?**
    Active listeners, empathic, fair, innovative, focused, and goal-oriented.
3   **What is the importance of possessing strong problem-solving skills?**
    Problem-solving allows us to determine solutions that elicit a win-win outcome for both people involved. Problem-solving promotes co-operation, collaboration, communication, and cohesion.

Activity 1: Amplify Assertiveness

•   Students will use the template below to complete this activity.
•   Stakeholders will give examples of scenarios that depict a problem/conflict
•   Stakeholders will discuss the importance of being assertive and standing up for oneself in a confident and straightforward manner rather than being passive (submissive) or aggressive (harsh and argumentative). Students will practice assertiveness skills by using "**I Messages**" in order to take ownership of their feelings and emotions.

Students must respond to each scenario using "I Messages." Students will follow the "I Message" template: I feel _____ when you _____ because_____. Using "I Messages" helps students to feel empowered by enabling them to problem solve in an autonomous way rather than deflecting or blaming others.

Scenario 1: A peer says a negative comment about you on social media
"I Message" Response:

_____

_____

Scenario 2: One of your best friends spread gossip about you
"I Message" Response:

_____

_____

Scenario 3: Your peers leave you out of a game during gym class
"I Message" Response:

_____

_____

Scenario 4: Your friend is making poor choices and wants you to follow along
"I Message" Response:

_____

_____

Scenario 5: A classmate is bullying you
"I Message" Response:

_____

_____

Activity 2: Helping Henry

- Stakeholders will divide students up into small groups.
- Henry is a special fish that cannot swim and his boat is stuck in the water.
- His oar is broken and needs the rescue team to save him so he does not drown in the rocky waters.
- The rescue team (the students) has to save Henry and place him back inside of his boat (the plastic cup).
- Henry is currently holding onto a rock (a ruler).
- One challenge is that the rescue team cannot touch, Henry, with their hands. The rescue team can only use the paper clips to rescue Henry.
- Henry cannot touch water (the desk) because he does not know how to swim
- Each group will receive two paper clips and a plastic cup.
- Students must work together and problem-solve in order to save Henry's life.

Follow-Up Questions:

In what ways is it important to possess problem-solving skills?
What steps can you take to improve your problem-solving skills?
In what ways did this activity help you to improve your problem-solving skills?

Group Feedback:

I enjoyed today's activity? ☺ or ☹

This activity helped me to understand the definition of problem-solving. ☺ or ☹

This activity helped me to understand the importance of possessing strong problem-solving skills. ☺ or ☹

Lesson Plan 4: Leadership

Lesson Plan Objective: To help students understand the definition of leadership, as well as the importance of possessing strong leadership skills.

Materials: Markers, Paper, Paper Plates, and Magazines

Group Questions:

1 **Ask students what the word leadership means**
    The action of leading a group of people in an effective manner
2 **Ask students what are some qualities that people with effective leadership possess?**
    Attentive listeners, flexible, cooperative, collaborative, team players
3 **What is the importance of possessing strong leadership skills?**
    Allows for efficiency and positive change.
4 **What does the word "Goal"mean?**
    It means working toward achieving something you would like to accomplish.
5 **What is the importance for leaders to set goals?**

That way they know what they are working toward and they stay focused.

Activity 1: Follow the Leader

* Students will work in dyads.
* One student will act as the follower and one student will act as the leader.
* The student acting as the follower must close his/her eyes or wear a blindfold and listen to what their partner tells them to draw.
* After five minutes, partners will then switch turns. Upon completion, students will debrief the experience in a large group.

Process Questions:

1 In what ways did this activity help you to improve your leadership skills?
2 What was the most challenging/rewarding aspect of this activity?
3 What qualities do you possess that will enable you to be an impactful leader?

Activity 2: Visionary Me
Use the template below to complete this activity

1 Indicate 3 strengths and inner resources you possess that make you an effective leader

   a
   b
   c

2 Based upon your strengths and inner resources, record three goals you want to achieve in the next week.
   Example: I want to get an A+ on my Spelling Test

   a
   b
   c

3 How do you feel when you set and achieve goals?
   _____
   _____

4 What are some steps you can take to achieve the goals you have set for yourself?

   a
   b
   c

5 Create a Vision Plate on a white paper plate using images/words illustrating the **three** goals you want to achieve in the next week.

Follow-Up Questions:

• In what ways is it important to possess leadership skills?
• What steps can you take to improve your leadership skills?
• Discuss the importance of setting goals?
• In what ways did this activity help you to improve your leadership skills?

Group Feedback:
I enjoyed today's activity? ☺ or ☹
This activity helped me to understand the definition of leadership. ☺ or ☹
This activity helped me to understand the importance of possessing strong leadership skills. ☺ or ☹

Lesson Plan 5: Friendship

Lesson Plan Objective: To help students understand the definition of friendship, as well as the importance of being a good friend.

Materials: Markers, Paper, Glue, and Hole Puncher, Elastic String, Colored Beads, Feathers, Masks, Glue, Glitter, Popsicle Sticks, Streamers, Upbeat Music.

Group Questions:

1   **Ask students what does the word friendship means?**
    The act of being friends, sharing common interests and values, as well as demonstrating and receiving mutual respect and acceptance.
2   **Ask students what are some qualities that people with strong friendship skills possess?**
    Compassionate, understanding, respectful, set boundaries, effective communicators, active listeners, thoughtful, and generous.
3   **What is the importance of possessing friendship skills?**
    Friendship allows for connectivity, understanding, collaboration, belonging, acceptance, purpose, and fulfillment.

Activity 1: Create a Mate Chain

* Stakeholders will pre-cut outlines of a human body prior to class/group
* Stakeholders will use a hole puncher to punch a hole in each of the human body outlines prior to giving them to students.
* On one side of the body template, students will record qualities that they believe a **good friend possesses.**
* On the other side of the template, students will record attributes that **they possess** that make them a good friend.
* Upon completion, stakeholders will assist students in creating a friendship chain.
* All cutouts will be placed next to one another and connected via ribbon (going through the hole punched area) making a circular chain that represents togetherness and inclusion.

Activity 2: Friendship Bracelets

* Students will work in small groups.
* Stakeholders will assist students in creating friendship bracelets using stretchy elastic and colored beads.
* Each color will represent a different quality or attribute
  Pink = Loving
  Orange = Kindness
  Yellow = Acceptance

Blue = Peace
Red = Understanding
Purple = Compassion
White = Respect
Green = Equality

- Students will make a beaded bracelet based upon the colors that they believe represent friendship, as well as the qualities they possess that are represented by each color.

Activity 3: Friendship Masquerade Ball

- Students will work in small groups.
- Students will create masquerade masks for a ball that they will have in class.
- Students will decorate the mask with attributes addressing the way that they see themselves as a friend, as well as the way in which they believe others perceive them as a friend.
- Students will use jewels, feathers, glitter, and markers to make their creations.
- Students will glue popsicle sticks on the back of their masks in order to hold them up for the masquerade ball.
- Upon completion, students will wear their masks to the "masquerade ball." Stakeholders will decorate the room with streamers and have upbeat music depicting friendship such as the song, "We Are Family," as students walk around and model their masks. ☺

Follow-Up Questions:
In what ways is it important to possess friendship skills?
In what ways did this activity help you to be mindful of the friendship skills you possess?
Indicate why we should include others …
Discuss the importance of being a good friend …
What steps can you take to be an even better friend?

Group Feedback:
I enjoyed today's activity? ☺ or ☹
This activity helped me to understand the definition of friendship. ☺ or ☹
This activity helped me to understand the importance of possessing strong friendship skills. ☺ or ☹

Lesson Plan 6: Optimism

Lesson Plan Objective: To help students understand the definition of optimism, as well as the importance of being an optimistic person.

Materials: Sharpie Markers, Paper, Magic Wand, Popsicle Sticks, Colored Ribbon, Stickers, Glitter, Glue.

Group Questions:

1   **Ask students what does the word optimism means?**
    The act of being positive, demonstrating hope, and confidence in the future.
2   **Ask students what are some qualities that optimistic people possess?**
    Hope, gratitude, positivity, strength, courage, resilience, belief, integrity, and bravery.
3   **What is the importance of being optimistic and positive in life?**
    Optimism allows for productivity, efficiency, goal achievement, perseverance, enhances self-efficacy, increases motivation, improves self-worth, as well as promotes striving toward self-actualization.
4   **What can people do to become more optimistic?**
    Belief in themselves, envision the future, set and achieve goals, state positive affirmations, positive self-talk, demonstrate self-love.

Activity 1: Magic Wand and Me
Students will record their responses to the following using the template below. Once students record their responses, stakeholders will provide the students with a magic wand that will be passed around to each student. Each student in the class/group will hold the magic while reading their responses to the following:

If a magic spell occurred and the problem you are facing went away, what in your life would be different and who would notice?

_____

_____

If you were granted a magical power, what steps would you take to overcome this challenge?

_____

_____

In what ways are you optimistic/positive about overcoming this challenge?

_____

_____

If you could grant **one** wish to yourself, what would this be?

_____

_____

How can staying positive help your wish to come true?

_____

_____

Activity 2: Gratitude Jar

- Students will individually create a Gratitude Jar using a plastic cup, Sharpie markers, and popsicle sticks.
- Students will record things/people/belongings in their lives that bring them a sense of hope and gratitude on the popsicle sticks using a Sharpie Marker.
- Students must record each topic on an individual popsicle stick.
- Students will decorate their gratitude jar with colored ribbons, glitter, stickers, and images that represent optimism, gratitude, and hope.

Follow-Up Questions:
Discuss the importance of being optimistic and having a positive mindset
In what ways does having a positive mindset enable us to show gratitude, appreciation, and be goal-oriented?
What steps can you take to be more optimistic and hopeful?

Group Feedback:
I enjoyed today's activity? ☺ or ☹
This activity helped me to understand the definition of optimism. ☺ or ☹
This activity helped me to understand the importance of demonstrating optimism. ☺ or ☹

References

Mattanah, J. F., Ayers, J. F., Brand, B. L., Brooks, L. J., Quimby, J. L., & McNary, S. W. (2010). A social support intervention to ease the college transition: Exploring main effects and moderators. *Journal of College Student Development, 51,* 92–108.

Weissberg, R. (2016). *Why social and emotional learning is essential for students.* Retrieved from https://www.edutopia.org/blog/why-sel-essential-for-students-weissberg-durlak-domitrovich-gullotta

19 Responsible Decision-Making

Responsible decision-making refers to making healthy decisions based upon considering ethical standards, morals, social norms, respect for others, choice-making, considering advantages and disadvantages, as well as ramifications of actions. This involves learning how to make constructive choices about personal behaviors and social interactions across various settings. It requires those to consider ethical standards, safety, norms, and being able to weigh out consequences of choices (Weissberg, 2016). According to Durlak, Weissberg, Dymnicki, Taylor, and Schellinger (2011), schools can teach social and emotional skills following the acronym SAFE including the following: (1) **Sequenced:** Connected and coordinated sets of activities that promote skill development. (2) **Active:** Active forms of learning that are experiential and help students learn and practice new skills. (3) **Focused:** Emphasis on developing personal and social skills. (4) **Explicit:** Targeting specific social and emotional learning skills. Responsible decision-making skills are imperative for graduates to attain, as they will have more independence, responsibility, and autonomy post-graduation and will be expected to make healthy choices in their own and others' best interest, regardless of their newfound freedom. Responsible decision-making involves the decision-making process, responsibility, negotiation, reflective practice, ethics, and assertiveness.

Secondary Activities

Lesson Plan 1: Leadership

Directions: This activity can be facilitated in a classroom, small group, or individual counseling setting. First, the definition of leadership will be addressed. Students will then process open-ended questions, complete the evidence-based practice activity, the creative activity, follow-up discussion questions in order to review material learned, as well as feedback questions to assess the impact of the session on student learning outcomes.

Definition of Leadership: Action of leading a group; acting as a leader or role model.

DOI: 10.4324/9781003262183-19

Open-Ended Questions:

In what ways is it important to be a leader or role model?
To set a positive example and to lead by example so that others can emulate positive behavior.

How does being a leader help to reduce bullying and aggression in schools?
Leaders help to create a positive school climate and set high expectations for others to treat one another with dignity and respect and to act in an appropriate and empathic manner.

What are steps that you can take to become a more impactful leader?
Believe in yourself, be the change you want to be, accept leadership roles, take initiative.

Evidence-Based Practice: Taking a strength-based approach, students will identify qualities and characteristics they possess that enable them to be effective leaders. Upon completion, each student will share their traits with their peers.

Creative Activity: Listen and Lead

- Leadership requires active and effective listening skills.
- Students will work in dyads.
- Each student will have the opportunity to act as the leader.
- The leader will delegate instructions and describe to their partner directions to follow.
- Partners will have to draw/illustrate exactly what the leader is instructing them to do and upon completion, switch turns
- Once both partners have the opportunity to act as the leader, process the following:
  - In what ways did this activity highlight the importance of active listening when taking on leadership roles?
  - What is the importance of delegating tasks when acting as a leader?
  - In what ways did this activity help to raise your self-awareness about the importance of possessing leadership qualities?

Discussion Questions
Share the significance of possessing leadership skills in order to create a safe and secure school climate …

How did these activities enable you to further augment your leadership skills?

What are some leadership roles you are interested in having in the future?

Discuss the leadership qualities that you further want to enhance in order to be a more impactful leader …

Feedback:
Counselors can either ask for verbal or written feedback in order to assess for impact of the session on student outcomes:

On a scale from one to five (1 being low and 5 being high) rate the following:

- This session helped to raise my awareness about leadership.
- This session helped me to recognize the impact that leadership has on my academic performance, social skills, and behaviors.
- This session helped me to recognize the skills I need to build in order to improve my leadership abilities.
- This session provided me with tools I can use to enhance my leadership skills.
- This session helped me to become more cognizant of the importance of effective leadership in order to have a safer and more secure school climate, as well as a productive workforce.

Lesson Plan 2: Accountability

Directions: This activity can be facilitated in a classroom, small group, or individual counseling setting. First, the definition of accountability will be addressed. Students will then process open-ended questions, complete the evidence-based practice activity, the creative activity, follow-up discussion questions in order to review material learned, as well as feedback questions to assess the impact of the session on student learning outcomes.

Definition of Accountability: Fact or condition of being accountable or responsible.
Open-Ended Questions:

What does accountability mean to you?
To take ownership and to be responsible
Discuss the importance for people to demonstrate accountability ...
To prevent deflecting, to look at one's role in a situation, as well as to make improvements—there is always room for growth.
Share what a teachable moment is ...
A life experience that one learns from and no matter the outcome, one is wiser and stronger as a result.
How does accountability help to reduce bullying/school violence?
    Accountability allows for self-reflection, taking ownership, responsibility, and demonstrating leadership, as well as assessing strengths and areas for growth, which helps to reduce bullying and school violence.

Evidence-Based Practice: Me, Myself, and I Reflective Practice

- Students will engage in reflective practice in order to assess strengths and areas of growth.
- Students will record a time in their lives when they blamed something on someone else rather than taking accountability.
- Students will record what they learned about themselves by going through the experience and what the outcome of the situation was.
- Students will record what they could have done differently in retrospect.

Creative Activity: Music and Me

- Music and lyrics are a powerful form of expression.
- Students will either think of a song or create lyrics of their own that highlight accountability.
- Students will then process ways in which the lyrics resonate with them in regard to the importance of demonstrating accountability.
- Students will also share the consequence of failing to demonstrate accountability and the impact that has on self and others.

Discussion Questions

In what ways does accountability help to create a more peaceful and secure school climate?

Share the importance of reflecting upon oneself in order to enhance accountability ...

In what ways did this activity help you to increase your understanding about the importance of demonstrating accountability?

What steps can you take moving forward in order to demonstrate greater accountability?

Feedback:

Counselors can either ask for verbal or written feedback in order to assess the impact of the session on student outcomes:

On a scale from one to five (1 being low and 5 being high) rate the following:

- This session helped to raise my awareness about accountability.
- This session helped me to recognize the impact that accountability has on my self-concept and choices.
- This session helped me to recognize steps that I can take in order to amplify my accountability.
- This session enabled me to enhance my accountability moving forward.

Elementary/Primary Activities to Become My Best SELf

Lesson Plan 1: Decision-Making Process

Lesson Plan Objective: To help students understand the definition of the decision-making process, the steps entailed, and the importance of being able to make good decisions.

Materials: Markers, Paper, Computer

Group Questions:

1. **What does the decision-making process mean?**
   The steps/process of making a good choice

2. **What steps arc involved in the decision-making process?**

Step 1 Identify the decision
Step 2 Gather information and weigh options
Step 3 Identify alternatives
Step 4 Weigh the evidence
Step 5 Choose among alternatives
Step 6 Take action and make your choice
Step 7 Review your decision and assess outcomes

3. **What is the importance of making healthy choices?**
Impacts our present and future, reinforces our judgment, improves self-concept, enhances autonomy, improves trust in oneself, and augments self-assurance.

Activity 1: So Many Choices My Oh My
Stakeholders will assist students in determining three decisions that students want to make. Students will follow the template, record their decisions, and provide responses to each of the seven decision steps in order to help them make methodical and sound choices

Step 1 **Identify the decision**
Step 2 **Gather information and weigh options**
Step 3 **Identify alternatives**
Step 4 **Weigh the evidence**
Step 5 **Choose among alternatives**
Step 6 **Take action and make your choice**
Step 7 **Review your decision and assess outcomes**

Decision 1

Step 1
Step 2
Step 3
Step 4
Step 5
Step 6
Step 7

Decision 2

Step 1
Step 2
Step 3
Step 4
Step 5
Step 6
Step 7

Decision 3

    Step 1
    Step 2
    Step 3
    Step 4
    Step 5
    Step 6
    Step 7

Activity 2: Making Decisions Contract

Stakeholders will assist students in developing a Making Decisions Contract. Students will record their responses to the following components using the template below. Upon completion, students will receive an Award of Excellence for effectively making a challenging decision

Dilemma: _____

Decision Needed By: _____ TODAY _____
Best Case Outcome:
_____
_____

Worst Case Outcome:
_____
_____

Advantages of Decision:
_____
_____

Disadvantages of Decision:
_____
_____

Heart Tells You To ...
_____
_____

Brain Tells You To ...
_____
_____

Final Decision:
_____
_____

Steps You Will Take to Put Decision in Action:

1
2
3

4

5

Follow-Up Questions:
What does the decision-making process entail?
Discuss the importance of being able to make good choices ...
What are some steps we can take to make healthy choices?

Group Feedback:
I enjoyed today's activity? ☺ or ☹
This activity helped me to understand the definition of the decision-making process. ☺ or ☹
This activity helped me to understand the importance of making healthy choices. ☺ or ☹

Award of Excellence

Name:

Date:

Ways Student Has Demonstrated Excellence:

Lesson Plan 2: Making Healthy Choices

Lesson Plan Objective: To help students understand the definition of decision-making and the importance of making healthy choices

Materials: Markers, Paper

Group Questions:

1. **Ask students what does the word decision-making means?**
   The action or process of making a decision/choice
2. **Ask students what are some qualities that people with healthy decision-making skills possess?**
   Rational, methodical, structured, organized, thoughtful, and aware
3. **What is the importance of possessing effective decision-making skills?**
   Able to make healthy choices that promote growth, as well as reduce indecision and impulsivity

Activity 1: Choices N' Consequences Activity
Stakeholders will read aloud a variety of scenarios. Students will then record the potential consequences involved in each scenario and circle whether it is a healthy or unhealthy choice on the template below. If the students indicate that a choice is unhealthy, they MUST indicate a healthier choice that could be made

Scenario 1: Your project is due tomorrow. Instead of starting it a few weeks ago, you wait until 7 PM the night before the due date to do your science project. You decide that you will complete it after you play with your friends.

Consequence:

_____

_____

Healthy Choice or Unhealthy Choice:

_____

_____

Scenario 2: You see someone being bullied on the bus. Rather than saying something, you ignore this behavior and wait quietly until you arrive at your bus stop.

Consequence:

_____

_____

Healthy or Unhealthy Choice:

_____

_____

Scenario 3: You are given a difficult math assignment. You are working hard to find the correct responses to the questions, but are struggling to understand the information. Rather than crumpling up your paper, you start tapping your leg and breathe deeply in and out five times.

Consequence:

_____

_____

Healthy or Unhealthy Choice:

_____

_____

Scenario 4: Your friend tells you something in confidence and asks you not to share the information with anyone else. By the end of the day, the entire class knows the information and your friend is ashamed, sad, and feels betrayed.

Consequence:

_____

_____

Healthy or Unhealthy Choice:

_____

_____

Activity 2: I Choose My Choice Activity
Stakeholders will assist students in recording three decisions that they need to make in the next week. Once students record their choices on the template below, they will then complete logical consequences

for each statement. **Logical Consequences** are vital in decision-making, as they help people list the pros and cons of their choices, helping them to make the best choice for themselves.

Decision 1:

_____

_____

Tell me what will happen if you do this:

_____

_____

Tell me what will happen if you do not do this:

_____

_____

Decision 2:

_____

_____

Tell me what will happen if you do this:

_____

_____

Tell me what will happen if you do not do this:

_____

_____

Decision 3:

_____

_____

Tell me what will happen if you do this:

_____

_____

Tell me what will happen if you do not do this:

_____

_____

Activity 3: Reflect to Perfect My Choices Activity
Stakeholders will assist students in recording their responses to the following on the template below

Indicate three examples of good choices

A
B
C

Indicate three examples of poor choices

A
B
C

One thing I have learned about making poor choices is ...

Complete the Stem:
When I made this poor choice to ...

_____

_____

The outcome was ...

_____

_____

In order to make better choices in the future, I will ...

_____

_____

Follow-Up Questions:
What does decision-making mean?
Discuss the importance of possessing decision-making skills
In what ways is it important to make healthy choices?

Group Feedback:
I enjoyed today's activity? ☺ or ☹
This activity helped me to understand the definition of decision-making.
☺ or ☹
This activity helped me to understand the importance of possessing effective decision-making skills. ☺ or ☹

Lesson Plan 3: Negotiation and Compromise

Lesson Plan Objective: To help students understand the definition of negotiation and compromise and the importance of both when making win–win decisions

Materials: Markers, Paper, Computer, and Monopoly Money

Group Questions:

1. **Ask students what does the word negotiation means?**
   The discussion is aimed at reaching an agreement.
2. **Ask students what compromise means ...**
   An agreement or settlement of a dispute that is reached when each side makes concessions/gives and takes.

3. **What is the importance of possessing effective negotiation/compromising skills?**
   To be able to collaboratively and cooperatively resolve an issue in a productive and efficient manner in order to have a positive outcome for both people involved in the dispute.
4. **Discuss the qualities that effective negotiators possess**
   Open, accepting, strong listening skills, respectful, positive, logical, and seek shared goals/outcomes, find the middle ground.

Activity 1: The Negotiators
Stakeholders will play the video and students will indicate the way in which the children in the video negotiated and came to a fair agreement.

https://www.youtube.com/watch?v=6ARqqqLSn4c

Students will record their responses to the following questions and debrief out loud ...
Record what this dispute is about

_____
_____
_____

Indicate the types of skills the children use to solve their problem

_____
_____
_____

Think about a dilemma you have faced. How did you resolve the dilemma?

_____
_____
_____

Describe the skills that you can use in the future to peacefully resolve a problem

_____
_____
_____

Activity 2: The Happiest Place on Earth

1 https://www.youtube.com/watch?v=qR2Urv5JvgM. In the movie, "Frozen," Hans had to use negation skills in order to make a deal. In what ways was negotiation used in this scene in order for Hans to have a win–win outcome?
2 https://www.youtube.com/watch?v=BV6EN4cm3UE. In the story, "The Little Mermaid," Ariel, trades her voice for the ability to walk on land and escape her life under the sea. Ariel had to leave her life and her family behind in hopes of experiencing life as a human rather than a mermaid. Is there anything that could have been done

differently in order for Ariel to experience a win–win outcome without her having to forego her existence as a mermaid?

3 https://www.youtube.com/watch?v=FNyfjWsyk2U. In the movie, "Beauty and the Beast," Belle decides to stay with the Beast in order to prevent her father from being kept as a prisoner. Is there anything else that could have been done differently in order for Belle to reach a win–win outcome without having her give up her freedom?

Activity 3: The Art of Negotiation

Stakeholders will work with students on negotiating and finding win–win resolutions to the following scenarios. Students will record their responses on the template below and share out loud.

Scenario 1

Your mom asks you to set the table while you are working on ABC Mouse.

Win–Win Resolution:

_____
_____
_____

Scenario 2

Your teacher asks you to come inside immediately after lunch. Students were promised a 20-minute recess.

Win–Win Resolution:

_____
_____
_____

Scenario 3

You want to stay outside with your friends and your parents are calling you in for dinner.

Win–Win Resolution:

_____
_____
_____

Scenario 4:

You want to stay up for 30-minutes watching your favorite Disney movie, but your parents want you to go to bed.

Win–Win Resolution:

_____
_____
_____

Scenario 5:

You want to have a strawberry flavored Pop-Tart with icing for breakfast and your mom wants you to eat eggs.

Win–Win Resolution:

_____

_____

_____

Activity 4: $ Shopping Trip at Target $

Stakeholders assist students on allocating how the money will be spent at Target. Students have $10 dollars to spend and they have different items that they need to buy in order to make a cake and clean up their mess afterward. Students need to negotiate with each other to figure out what items they MUST have in order to bake a cake that they all will eat and clean up afterward.

Items We Must Buy:

1

2

3

4

5

Items We Are Willing to Forego:

1

2

3

4

5

How did it feel knowing you could not buy everything you wanted?

_____

_____

_____

What is the importance of negotiating in order to make a healthy choice?

_____

_____

Follow-Up Questions:

What did you learn about the art of negotiation?

What was the most challenging/rewarding part of this activity?

What is the importance of negotiation?

Small-Group Feedback:

I enjoyed today's activity? ☺ or ☹

This activity helped me to understand the definition of negotiation and compromise. ☺ or ☹

This activity helped me to understand the importance of possessing effective negotiation skills. ☺ or ☹

Lesson Plan 4: Reflective Practice

Lesson Plan Objective: To help students understand the definition of reflective practice and the importance of engaging in reflective practice in order to reach one's fullest potential.

Materials: Markers, Paper, Legos, Waffles, Marbles, Pasta, Play-Doh, and Paper Clips, Ribbon, Feathers, Pom Poms, Rubber Bands

Group Questions:

1. **Ask students what does the word reflective practice means?**
   To engage in continuous self-evaluation in order to understand one's actions, reactions, strengths, areas for growth, as well as working toward self-improvement (Farrell, 2012).
2. **Which of the six steps of the reflective practice cycle do you believe is most important?**

   Step 1 Description: What happened?
   Step 2 Feelings: What did you think and feel about it?
   Step 3 Evaluation: What were the positives and negatives?
   Step 4 Analysis: What sense can you make of it?
   Step 5 Conclusion: What else could you have done?
   Step 6 Action Plan: What will you do next time?

3. **What is the importance of engaging in reflective practice?**
   To be able to problem-solve, to identify areas of strength and areas for improvement, to determine what steps need to be taken to make improvements, to promote motivation and goal achievement, to encourage us to reach our fullest potential.
4. **Discuss the qualities that people with reflective practice skills possess:**

Insightful, self-aware, tenacious, motivated, flexible, willing, think critically, as well as have a desire to change and improve.

Activity 1: Read to Achieve Magnificence
Stakeholders will read the book, '*The Most Magnificent Thing*' https://www. amazon.com/Most-Magnificent-Thing-Ashley-Spires/dp/1554537045/ref=sr_ 1_1?s=books&ie=UTF8&qid=1531524846&sr=1-1&keywords=the+most +magnificent+thing&smid=ATVPDKIKX0DER
Upon completion, students will record their responses to the following and share them out loud:

What is the moral of this story?

_____
_____
_____

Indicate how the young girl is engaged in critical thinking and reflective practice:

_____

_____

_____

What is the consequence in life when we get frustrated and decide to quit?

_____

_____

_____

Describe the importance of striving to improve and working to be the best version of yourself ...

_____

_____

_____

Activity 2: Lego My Eggo Castle

Directions:

- Students will be given various materials to build a castle using Legos.
- Stakeholders can be there to support the students, but are encouraged to ask students, "What do you think?" rather than answering their questions immediately.
- Students will be placed in small groups and given 20 minutes to build a **castle** out of Legos, Eggo Mini Waffles, and other materials including pasta, marbles, paper clips, and Play-Doh.
- As students are building their castles, stakeholders can ask the following questions to students to assist them in building and enhancing reflection and critical thinking skills ...

1 **How can we think about building this castle in a different way?**
2 **Which material gives the castle a strong foundation?**
3 **What are some other ways you can construct this castle?**
4 **If you had other materials available, what other materials could you use to build this castle?**
5 **What has been the most challenging and rewarding part of building your castle together?**

Upon completion, ask students to respond to the following out loud ...

- In what ways did you think critically while completing the castle?
- Upon reflection, what do you believe was effective about your construction of the castle, as well as what you could improve?

- What can you do differently in the future to build an even larger and sturdier castle?

Activity 3: Me, Myself, and I

Students will record their strengths, areas for growth, as well as steps students can take to turn their areas for improvement into a strength using the template below.

My Top Five Strengths ...

1
2
3
4
5

My Top Five Areas for Growth

1
2
3
4
5

Steps I Can Take to Turn My Areas for Improvement Into Strengths ...

Area for Improvement 1:

_____

A
B
C

Area for Improvement 2:

_____

A
B
C

Area for Improvement 3:

_____

A
B
C

Area for Improvement 4:

_____

A
B
C

Area for Improvement 5:

_____

A
B
C

Activity 4: Genie in a Bottle

- Stakeholders will provide students with empty plastic cups and materials (pom poms, feathers, rubber bands, ribbons, cotton balls, paper clips).
- Students will have 10–15 minutes to fill the cups with materials, objects, and colors that represent **areas for growth**, as well as their **strengths.**
- Students will then present their Genie in a Bottle cups to the class/group and share the following:
- Reasons for including their chosen materials
- Steps that they can take to turn their areas for growth into strengths

Follow-Up Questions:
What did you learn about the importance of critical thinking?
Discuss the significance of engaging in reflective practice (identifying strengths and weaknesses) ...
Indicate the importance of making continuous self-improvements ...

Group Feedback:
I enjoyed today's activity? ☺ or ☹
This activity helped me to understand the definition of reflective practice and critical thinking. ☺ or ☹
This activity helped me to understand the importance engaging in reflective practice and thinking critically. ☺ or ☹

Lesson Plan 5: Ethics and Morality

Lesson Plan Objective: To help students understand the definition of ethics and morals and the importance of acting in an ethical and moral manner.

Materials: Markers, Paper, and Poster Board

Group Questions:

1. **What does the word ethics mean?**
   Moral principles that govern one's behaviors and choices.
2. **What does the word morals mean?**
   Standards and principles to live by, particularly discerning right from wrong.
3. **What is the importance of acting in an ethical and moral manner?**
   It leads us to be humane citizens who value the rules that society must abide by, in order to be trustworthy individuals who act responsibly and make healthy choices.
4. **Discuss the qualities that people with morals and ethics possess** pride, listening skills, respectful, humble, cognizant, law abiding, empathic, and have effective decision-making skills.

Activity 1: Tell the Truth the Whole Truth and Nothing but the Truth
Stakeholders will read the book, *"Ruthie and the Not So Teeny Tiny Lie"*
https://www.amazon.com/gp/product/1599900106/ref=as_li_tl?ie=UTF8&
camp=1789&creative=9325&creativeASIN=1599900106&linkCode=as2&
tag=pts08-20&linkId=aa114672e82e2a5d074b0ba2b66963a9
What is the moral of this story?

_____

_____

Indicate the qualities that this young girl possessed.

_____

_____

What are some consequences we face when we tell a lie and are dishonest?

_____

_____

Describe the importance of telling the truth and being honest ...

_____

_____

What lesson did Ruthie learn at the end of the story?

_____

_____

Activity 2: GooGoo and Yaya
Students will watch the video. Students will then record responses to the following questions and share them out loud.
https://www.youtube.com/watch?v=4U3ED-iG2Uw

1 In what ways was GooGoo dishonest in the video?

_____

_____

2 How did you know GooGoo was being dishonest?

_____

_____

3 What happens when we blame others for our actions rather than be honest?

_____

_____

4 Indicate the importance of making mistakes.

_____

_____

5 Discuss the significance of learning from our mistakes.

_____

_____

Activity 3: Manners and Etiquette
Directions: On a large piece of poster paper, using neon Sharpie Markers, stakeholders and students will brainstorm about the different types of manners that we use in general, with adults, with friends, and at home in order to enhance moral and ethical behavior. Students will identify and record appropriate manners and etiquette to use in the following situations:

In General:

_____

_____

With Teachers:

_____

_____

With Parents:

_____

_____

With Peers:

_____

_____

At Home:

_____

_____

On the Bus:

_____

_____

At Recess:

_____

_____

Upon completion, ask students to verbally respond to the following:

- In what ways is it important to use manners?
- How do we feel when someone treats us unethically?
- What are things we can do to act more morally and ethically?

Activity 4: To Be or Not To Be … Honest

Students will record responses to the following on the template below:

- On the template below, students will **draw** what honesty looks like to them and **name** their image depicting honesty.
- On the template below students will **draw** what a lie looks like to them and **name** their image depicting a lie.
- Students will record a time in their lives when they were dishonest.
- Students will indicate the outcome of the situation.
- Students will indicate the emotions they experienced when lying.
- Students will indicate what lesson they learned as a result of telling a lie.
- Students will indicate the qualities that they possess that make them honest.
- Students will indicate what they can do in the future to continue demonstrating morality and honesty.

To Be or not to be Honest…Template

1 On one side of a blank piece of paper, draw an image of honesty and indicate a name for honesty
2 On the other side of the blank piece of paper, draw an image of a lie and indicate a name for the lie
3 A time in your life when you were dishonest:

_____

_____

4 Outcome of the situation:

_____

_____

5 Emotions experienced when telling a lie:

_____

_____

6 Lesson learned from telling a lie:

_____

_____

7 Qualities you possess that make you honest:

_____

_____

8 Steps you can take in the future to demonstrate greater morality and honesty

_____

_____

Follow-Up Questions:
Discuss the importance of acting in a moral and ethical manner ...
Indicate the significance of making moral and ethical choices ...
In what ways is it important to be honest and to tell the truth?
Small-Group Feedback:
I enjoyed today's activity? ☺ or ☹
This activity helped me to understand the definition of ethics and morals.
☺ or ☹
This activity helped me to understand the acting in an ethical, moral, and honest manner. ☺ or ☹

Lesson Plan 6: Cultural Responsiveness

Lesson Plan Objective: To help students understand the definition of cultural responsiveness and the importance of demonstrating cultural responsiveness and acceptance of others

Materials: Markers, Paper

Group Questions:

1. **What does it mean to be culturally responsive?**
   The ability to learn from and relate to others respectfully with people from your own culture, as well as those from different cultures.
2. **What is the importance of demonstrating cultural responsiveness?**
   This allows us to understand, relate to, connect with, collaborate with, and celebrate others who share similar and different cultures, values, ideologies, and beliefs.
3. **How can we be culturally responsive at school?**
   Create a class that is open, inclusive, engaging, understanding, respectful, celebrates culture, promotes sharing, discussion, and unconditional acceptance for all.
4. **Discuss the qualities that culturally sensitive people possess**

Intelligent, knowledgeable, open-minded, flexible, tolerant, accepting, perceptive, inquisitive, empathic, and nonjudgmental.

Activity 1: Dare to be Different

Stakeholders will read the book, *"It's Ok To Be Different"*
https://www.amazon.com/Its-Okay-Different-Todd-Parr/dp/0316043478/
ref=as_li_ss_tl?s=books&ie=UTF8&qid=1501618527&sr=1-1&keywords
=its+okay+to+be+different&linkCode=sl1&tag=wear03e-20&linkId=fe
6278ce0f06132dcf100c24322fcf7d

What is the moral of this story?

_____

_____

Indicate the importance of being understanding and accepting of others
who are different from us ...

_____

_____

Discuss the importance of being proud of who we are ...

_____

_____

In what ways can we demonstrate greater acceptance and cultural sensitivity toward others?

_____

_____

Activity 2: Jam to Acceptance

https://www.youtube.com/watch?v=oODXem4oRp0

Upon completion, students will verbally discuss the following out loud

- What is the meaning of this song?
- What is the importance of being proud of the color of our skin?
- Indicate the emotions we feel when we experience acceptance ...
- Discuss the significance of loving ourselves and respecting others who
  are similar and different from us?
- What are some ways we can be more accepting of others?

Activity 3: Kiddos Around the World

**Stakeholders will hang up a map of the world and students will complete the
following using the template below:**

- Each student in the class will create a caricature of themselves and
  place a popsicle stick on the back of their caricature.
- Students will draw their caricature based upon their **cultural background.**
- Students will place their caricature on the country on the map of the
  world that their family originally comes from.
- Students will also record responses to the questions on the template
  below and share their responses with the class/group.

- Stakeholders will decorate their classroom/office with the map of the world along with the students' written responses in order to create a unique, celebratory, inclusive and culturally responsive classroom.

Kiddos Around the World Template

1 Create a caricature of yourself based upon your culture of origin and place a popsicle stick behind your caricature in order to hold it up and share your uniqueness with the world
2 Food within my cultureI love to eat:

_____

_____

3 Values within my culture that I value:

_____

_____

4 Beliefs within my culture that I believe:

_____

_____

5 Three things I love about my culture:

_____

_____

A
B
C

The most special part about being from my culture is ...

_____

_____

One thing I want others to know about my culture is ...

_____

_____

Activity 4: Circle of Culture, Peace, Love, and Happiness

Stakeholders will assist students with tracing and cutting out an outline of their hand and forearm. Students will then do the following:

- Color the image of the forearm and hand with colors and images that represent their culture of origin.
- On the hand, write down the name of the country/countries that their ancestors came from.
- On the forearm, write down **three** qualities that they possess that makes them different and special ☺

Upon completion, stakeholders will then glue all of the hands together and place in their classroom/office to create a culturally responsive climate

Activity 5: Chugga Chugga Choo Choo Chocolate and Apples MMM MMM Good

Directions:

- Stakeholders will provide each student with different colored apples (red, yellow, green, multicolor).
- Stakeholders will also provide 10 M&Ms to students comprised of various colors.
- Stakeholders will instruct students to take a bite of their apple along with biting into several different colored M&Ms.

Upon completion, students will record responses to the following and share out loud ...
What was the moral of this activity?

_____

_____

What did you notice about the inside of the apples and M&Ms despite being different colors on the outside?

_____

_____

In what ways does this activity relate to people?

_____

_____

What can we do to recognize that we are more alike than we are different and celebrate ourselves/one another?

_____

_____

Follow-Up Questions:

What did you learn about the importance of being culturally responsive? Discuss the significance of demonstrating self-respect and respect toward others who are different from us ...
Indicate the importance of treating everyone equally, honestly, and celebrating similarities and differences ...

Group Feedback:

I enjoyed today's activity? ☺ or ☹
This activity helped me to understand the definition of cultural responsiveness. ☺ or ☹
This activity helped me to understand the importance of celebrating diversity and being accepting and respectful toward everyone. ☺ or ☹

References

Durlak, J. A., Weissberg, R. P., Dymnicki, A. B., Taylor, R. D., & Schellinger, K. B. (2011). The impact of enhancing students' social and emotional learning: A meta-analysis of school-based universal interventions. Child Development, 82(1), 405–432. Retrieved from http://casel.org/wp-content/uploads/Meta-Analysis-Child-Development-Full-Article1.pdf

Weissberg, R. (2016). *Why social and emotional learning is essential for students.* Retrieved from https://www.edutopia.org/blog/why-sel-essential-for-students-weissberg-durlak-domitrovich-gullotta

20 The End or the New Beginning

Even during a time of intense division and opposition in our country, school stakeholders and society at large must come together to unify on this topic: Ending Violence in Schools. Regardless of political ideology, religious beliefs, gender, sexuality, socioeconomic status, or race, ALL human beings fundamentally want to live in a safe society. ALL human beings want their children going to school, getting educated, improving academically, socially emotionally, behaviorally, and vocationally so that future generations can have an even better life. This is universal. Although school violence is a complex issue, there is true simplicity here: all human beings want their children to come home safely, intact, wiser, braver, more knowledgeable, and stronger once school is dismissed.

Every day is a new day to learn, grow, engage in self-awareness, and self-reflection. Although there is no manual or blueprint to implicitly ending school violence, we do know this: implementing antibullying programs, incorporating social emotional learning (SEL), and increasing mental health awareness, access, and resources are **nonnegotiable**. These **three** entities **must** be in place in order to create safer, more secure, and healthier school climates that are conducive to student learning, growth, empowerment, triumphs, and survival. We cannot have one (school safety) without the other (SEL, antibullying, and mental health resources). Maslow's Hierarchy of Needs stated that in order to self-actualize, one must have their physiological needs, safety needs, experience love, and belonging, have esteem for self and others; all of these entities allow one to then become the best version of themselves. Although full self-actualization does not occur, as there is always learning and growth, the process becomes possible.

Educators, key stakeholders, and family members need to affirm and teach students: They are Wise. They are Brave. They are Strong. They are Fierce. They are Smart. They are Beautiful. They are Supported. They are Brave. They are Resilient. They are Able. They Can Achieve Their Dreams. Anything Is Possible. They are Worthy. They are the Future. They are Loved. They are Unstoppable. It is incredible what students can do when stakeholders show their perpetual belief in them; they then have everlasting

DOI: 10.4324/9781003262183-20

belief in themselves. It takes one person to truly make a lasting difference. There is no greater reward or gift than to be able to pay forward all of our life experiences in order to generate promise, safety, and optimism for future generations. That is priceless. As bullying and revenge are the two leading causes for school violence, eradicating bullying and helping students to become assertive, proactive, empathic, leaders, accountable, effective communicators, listeners, problem solvers, and regulators are instrumental for peace, prosperity, love, and light. Although this reference guide is coming to an end; it is really a new beginning, as we now are mindful of the profound power of SEL and the positive impact it has on academic performance, social and emotional skills, career readiness, and mental health wellness. We have identified steps that schools can take, topics that schools can address, strategies that schools can use, as well as programs and interventions that schools can implement in order to amplify safety, prosperity, equality, security, connectivity, unconditional acceptance, and infinite hope.

Index

For Product Safety Concerns and Information please contact our EU
representative GPSR@taylorandfrancis.com
Taylor & Francis Verlag GmbH, Kaufingerstraße 24, 80331 München, Germany

www.ingramcontent.com/pod-product-compliance
Lightning Source LLC
Chambersburg PA
CBHW070325270326
41926CB00017B/3770